CHISPAS

TENDING THE SACRED FLAME IN CHILDREN

A Toolkit for Families, Educators, & Community Members
of Nature-based Education Programs

By Meag Diamond

Founder and director of Chavitos Nature Program

Chispas: A Toolkit for Families, Educators, & Community Members of Nature-based Education Programs by Meag Diamond

Cover Design & Layout by Chris Adams
Editing by Pinnacle Text & Ease Ally

Portions of the land acknowledgement used in this book, particularly text written in the Twulshootseed language, are from the Puyallup Tribal Language Program website. The mission of this program is, "to be kind, be helpful and be sharing in terms of revitalizing the Twulshootseed language by producing language users." We thank the Puyallup Tribal Language Program for the use of this valuable resource. Find out more about the Puyallup Tribal Language Program at puyalluptriballanguage.org.

Vega Books, an Imprint of Blue Cactus Press | caləɬali

Acknowledgement

ʔukʼʷədiid čəł ʔuhigʷəd txʷəl tiił ʔa čəł ʔal tə swatxʷixʷtxʷəd ʔə tiił puyaləpabš. ʔa ti dxʷʔa ti swatxʷixʷtxʷəd ʔə tiił puyaləpabš ʔəsłatałlil tulʼal tudiʔ tuhaʔkʷ. didiʔł ʔa həlgʷəʔ ʔal ti sləx̌il. dxʷəsłatłlils həlgʷəʔ gʷəl X̌ʼuyayus həlgʷəʔ gʷəl X̌ʼuX̌ʼax̌ʷad həlgʷəʔ tiił bədədəʔs gʷəl tix̌dxʷ həlgʷəʔ tiił ʔiišəds həlgʷəʔ gʷəl X̌ʼuʔalalus həlgʷəʔ gʷəl X̌ʼutxʷəlšucidəb. x̌ʷəla···b ʔə tiił tuyəlʼyəlabs.

Blue Cactus Press is located in caləłali, on puyaləpabš land. This land was stolen and colonized by settlers via the signing of the Treaty of Medicine Creek in 1854. Since then, it has not been returned to its rightful and traditional stewards, puyaləpabš, also known as the Puyallup Tribe of Indians.

We acknowledge that we benefit from our existence at caləłali. We are thankful to live, work, and be in relationship with the land and people here.

Contents

A Note on Positionality & Privilege

I want to take a moment to start by acknowledging my privilege. Growing up, my family was middle class. My dad and stepmom were successful leaders and managers for curriculum companies like National Geographic and Houghton Mifflin Harcourt. They both started their careers as teachers, gradually working their way up to management positions. As a result of their success, my family lived in a big house surrounded by other big homes in Tigard, Oregon. After my parents separated, I remained with my mother and lived with my father every other weekend. My mother became a single mom working three jobs as an elementary librarian, a peach vendor at the summer farmer markets, and a public librarian on the weekends. Money was handled differently in both my mom and dad's house. While I always had what I needed in both homes, I knew money came from a lot of hard work and long hours in the workplace.

My privilege of inherited wealth made me feel secure enough to take risks in my life. After leaving home as a young adult, embarking on my own, I worked as a public-school teacher and began preparing to travel to Africa. I had zero dollars in my bank account and my cabinets were almost always empty, except for a bag of cornmeal and preserved cherries. Despite this, my community at the time supported me when I was in need. They picked me up from the mechanic when my car broke down (with a bag of groceries in the backseat) and a friend stuffed some money under my apartment door every now and then. Community saved me plenty of times. Because I felt secure enough to take risks, I sold everything I owned and moved to Africa. Later, I moved to different countries to pursue my dreams of supporting orphans. Throughout my adult life, I have lived without fear of poverty because I have always had a safety net to catch me if I fell. And I fell, many times.

In 2013 I married my husband, Jose. His own story, and the privilege he holds, are very different from my own. He was born in rural Guatemala. His grandma raised him while his mom worked in the city. With no electricity or running water, his young childhood wasn't spent playing, but instead, collecting wood and contributing to household stability. When I met him, he was volunteering in Guatemala at Safe Passage. His life was more economically stable because of the sacrifices that his mom and stepdad made later, during his young adult life. When I met him, as an adult, he too had become a risk taker and status quo breaker. He lived on his own and had a teaching job covered by a grant. However, he was still underemployed, working twelve-hour days six days a week. He had built up a small savings that he kept under his mattress (which was later stolen) and supported his family with his income. When he immigrated to the United States, he had one suitcase to his name and no other assets. Since then, he has benefitted from the privilege that comes from marrying an American.

It's partly our privilege that lets us — Jose and I — take risks with our future and our professions. But it's also our mindset. We both save money by using our skill sets, bartering for goods and services, and asking for community support when we need it. We have one car that Jose regularly fixes. We have a home in a safe neighborhood, though we couldn't afford it if we didn't rent out the basement-level as an apartment. We own a farm, but lease it out to farmers of queer, neurodiverse and immigrant identities who will grow their own ancestral foods to serve the community. We value offering this intentional support, even though doing so barely covers the mortgage. We built our mother, who lives in Guatemala, a new home of earthbags when hers had become threadbare, drafty and wobbly. We built it with our hands, and with those of friends who needed jobs to support their growing families in the indigenous village of San Lucas

Toliman, near Lake Atitlan. All of this to say, we've been blessed with abundance, but to enjoy it, we must lean heavily on our skill sets, sweat equity, and community support. When we can, we like to use our resources and wealth to bless others. I'm grateful for currently living a secure life, and we know that if that ever changes (again), we will have community and support from those around us.

Part 1

Preparation

Chapter 1
Reconnect With Your Intuition

There I was, living in a Guatemalan rainforest at the foot of a volcano. Lake Atitlan was blue and alive from my view on our patio. I paused and watched the birds living their best lives in the outstretched branches of the amate tree, which, in that moment, provided me with shade. I experienced a rare moment: our stone roundhouse was silent. My kids and husband were at school in La Puerta Abierta. I had stayed home, sensing I could do my work in silence. I didn't want to take the 30-minute, winding car ride to school that day to drop off the kids. As I sat on the bench overlooking the lake, something quieted in me. We — my family and I — had been living in this rural Guatemalan village for a few months. I had detoxed from the frazzled life of being a director at our nature school. My internet was unreliable, and my main daily chores reduced to laundry and tidying.

My needs had been met, and a shift began to happen within. No longer was the grind of everyday life yapping in my ear or a to-do list tapping me on the shoulder. My needs for food, like fresh eggs and vegetables, now came from local indigenous farmers and neighbors, and peace and safety for my family had been secured. The shift began as a faint whisper in my mind and body. It was distant yet familiar, and it was stirring and responding to the changes we had made in our family's life. I nodded my head to the energy in greeting, which bolstered it, encouraging it to speak a little louder. A corner of my heart started to warm and came back to life. With this permission and encouragement, the voice grew louder and started to share stories and wisdom. A deep part of my mind was caressed, and started to shift, as if stretching out its weak and underused muscles. A great transformation was taking place inside me, and magic was awakening me to the process of re-trusting my inner animal instincts.

This re-trusting was the beginning of reconnecting with my intuition, my heart's call, my deep desires, my animal wisdom, and ancient knowledge. It was a remembering of stories and a lifestyle so different from the one people are told to march obediently to. *And I liked it.* At the time, we were staying in Guatemala because that is where my husband was born and raised. Before we got married, and after I became pregnant, he decided to move to Tacoma, Washington. Eleven months later, we were married. Ever since then, it was always my goal to live in Guatemala for six months out of the year.

In hindsight, this re-trusting and reconnecting with the energy inside me was a major turning point. We had already taken the decision to turn from traditional schooling and family roles. We had started our school and were successfully growing each year. This was the year when I decided to take back my story and narrative from the toxic social media expectations and deflated values of our American society.

As I listened to what I call Spirit, I scribbled notes in my journal and followed rabbit trails lined with serendipity and synchronicity. I had tasted what a slower day felt like. I had nibbled on the possibility of having a daily rhythm that included spaciousness and quietude. I had seen what wisdom sprang into my mind from making time to observe the waters of a healing lake and the moody clouds that swept in over the volcano mountaintops. I took those learnings, tucked them into my suitcase of clothing and gifts for family, and brought them back to Tacoma when our six months were over.

Once I was back in the U.S., the wisdom of slowing down helped me reorganize my day. Instead of having a rushed morning, I decided to carve out three hours of administration time each day. This included a morning neighborhood walk, a cup of mushroom tea, and a daily meditation and journaling ritual to help boost my gratitude and get me started with a mindset of awe and wonder. When we nod towards that faint whisper of forgotten wisdom in this way, when we lean in towards the tug of a new sprout of an idea, when we remain soft and curious about an observation, we are listening to our intuition. We are tuning into a frequency only available to those who are vulnerable, listening with heart, and expecting sacredness.

Five years later, I thank goddess for those schedule changes we made when we returned to the U.S. Not only because it has guided me to make the changes mentioned above but because it has also guided decisions around my business. Otherwise, I might still be stuck on a path and rat race that I didn't even know I was participating in. I'm never turning back.

I believe when we listen deeply and trust our inner voice, we make better choices, we live more aligned to our values, and we are more inclined to follow our higher calling in life. You can do this too if you awaken your intuition and inner voice. Trust the process of realignment. It doesn't take living in Guatemala for six months. It can happen right where you are, and in this very moment.

To help you begin this process of re-trusting your inner voice and needs, here are some practices that might help you hear. Consider starting by allowing yourself to be in silence more often. In the car driving, on a run, or eating breakfast, instead of plugging in a podcast or reaching for your phone, don't. Just enjoy your bagel or drive in silence. Be alone with your thoughts. We can't hear if we have too many inputs all nagging for our attention. Truth be told, humans aren't made to multitask. It robs us of truly experiencing the main task we are doing.

Also, surround yourself with teachers, those mentors who have the strong ability to listen deeply. They will bring confirmation to those times you hear something fresh and new. Spirit will bring confirmation through other teachings and events. Intuition is a muscle that needs to be built, and it will take practice. Honor the whispers and glimmers by writing them down. This is a signal to Spirit that you are ready for more and that the beginning connection is ready to strengthen. May your journey be filled with courage and encouragement.

Returning to my personal story of slowing down and getting quiet, I admit, it is not the norm or average way of life in this modern world. We live in an era dominated by disconnection and distraction. A time of numbing our feelings so we can keep going and producing. A time of expectations of having busy, buzzing minds to match our equally chaotic and frenzied time schedules and deadlines. We live in a culture that highly values and praises the ability to produce, admiring those who proudly hold up a completed to-do list, 100 tasks accomplished, propped up like some victory banner waving over their weary-to-the-bone bodies.

I long for the culture where these expectations are absurd and laughable, too ridiculous to even entertain. One where the focus is on connecting with people in our communities, noticing and tending to plants for nourishment and medicine, and honoring the close interconnectedness to blessed land, as it is what sustains us. Unfortunately, technology and speed are our gods now. Meaning, we walk with bowed heads in reverence, with our eyes tuned into the images flashing on our screen. Little beeps and dings demanding and calling away our attention. We've all witnessed pedestrians on a city street bump into each other or get woken by a blasting honk from a car just feet away from them, jarring them back into the moment and life happening away from their screen. Mere seconds later, after they've assessed their safety, their eyes return back to their demanding screens. Our addiction to technology is pervasive and consuming in this way. We connect with our phones as easily as we connect our phones to a power source. We know the names of apps and celebrities but can't identify local birds or plants and don't know the names of our neighbor across the street who walks his dog every day at 5:00 a.m. on the dot. We also don't really know how certain foods make our bodies feel. We take highways to zip from city to city, skipping the scenic route, trying to beat rush hour. We sit in rush hour as solo drivers, surrounded by other commuters heading to the same suburbs. We eat food sprayed and packaged countless miles away by those nameless faces whose story we don't care to know, as long as the food is cheap and convenient. Food labels are paragraphs of words we can't even pronounce. Processed foods make us obese. Our bodies are deficient in minerals and vitamins, so we supplement with medications that have side effects which outweigh the benefits. Yet, we are unaware that these are all side effects of living a life disconnected and out of tune with our bodies' deep and innate needs. Humans have had the same needs since time immemorial. But we've strayed so far from the simple solutions presented in lessons learned from watching nature that we don't remember what our needs are.

Gratefully, some of us remember, some of us are recalling, some of us are waking to the feeling of emptiness and starting to question. My intention in this book is to tell you this is good and to encourage you to acknowledge and listen to those feelings. I want to offer my own story as an example of what you can accomplish if you do so. What you can change in your life if you follow those soft inclinations. I offer my story as an example of a possible outcome. Understand that this work will look different for each of us. May we all start to ask ourselves; *how do we give less power to outside sources that don't want the best for us? How do we return to a lifestyle that is more nourishing and heart-driven?*

As you start to listen to your intuition, remember, Gaia is the best mentor, teacher, and guide there is. Gaia is the earth. She comes from ancient stories told in almost every culture if we search far enough back. There is a way for those who want to reestablish the connection between our psyche and our body, between ourselves and others, and between humanity and the earth. We must return to the natural cycles of the earth. No matter where any one person is on their journey of realigning to natural cycles, it's important to remember that we all have the opportunity to reteach ourselves to do so. We can learn how to trust ourselves again by listening and observing nature.

Fast forward nine years and the process of intuiting the next steps continues. Just this past month, my husband and I were restarting this realignment process with our K-8 program, which we've been building for the past three years. While our preschool was constructed with relative ease, the K-8 program has come with a lot of toil and struggle. I share this so you know that the process of building and using your intuition isn't all roses and rainbows. There is also hard work involved. This year, I often felt constricted and grumpy around some of my responsibilities as a leader and director. These emotions called me to notice and lean in. Why wasn't I enjoying my job anymore? Where did we lose the ease? Were we still on the right path? Were any of the lessons from our past repeating? Were there deeper parts of my being and leadership that needed to be healed or examined? Is any of this specific struggle due to bigger systems of racism and sexism? What lessons did I need to learn from these experiences, and how could I use this wisdom to help guide others wanting to start a nature school? I had so many questions.

If I didn't already maintain a strong practice of meditation, intuition and creating spaciousness to slow down and listen, I think quitting would have been a logical choice during this reflection period. But, when I played around with that possibility of quitting, I felt dis-ease and jarred. With one child starting middle school and the other entering second grade, I was highly motivated to keep them in alternative education. At the same time, the faces of all the other students who were thriving in our program also crossed my mind. We decided to keep our K-8 program open and running. This decision didn't stop the questions, however. It spurred new questions that I needed to entertain. Like the whack-a-mole game, one question was down, but three more popped up. So, my listening process started over again, with new questions to help guide us forward. I felt Spirit teaching me about multifunctional relationships. So, who was supposed to be on our Chavitos team? Which relationships felt draining and difficult, like I was walking knee high in oozy sludge? Which ones were filling multiple purposes and sparking vision and zeal? How could we realign or restructure our K-8 program to alleviate the exhaustion, constriction, and frustrations I felt? What parts of being a director did I not want to do anymore? What were my favorite director's responsibilities? Who in my life could I call upon for support and share responsibilities with? How do I shift my mindset of Jose and I being "saviors" and solution finders at the school to sharing the burden and having this co-op system really work? How could we move toward community empowerment? Endless questions wracked my mind.

Answering all of them meant I would need to go through a significant amount of listening to my body and noticing where and when exhaustion was happening. Exhaustion is not my normal state; it's a position of misalignment for me. It's not sustainable and doesn't align with my picture of vitality and thriving. Any time I am feeling out of synchronicity it usually involves the heaviness of exhaustion. It's one of my indicators to pause. I also paid attention to when I got goosebumps, awoke with a new idea, or the flow of a solution felt easy and light. It's important to ask ourselves, what emotions and feelings are my telltale sign that I am going in the right direction and making aligned choices?

Finding the answers to these questions was like finding the keys to unlock doors of possibility. The answers let us be more honest about what was not giving us life. With these answers, I felt like I could figure out the code to my prosperity as it related to work. Now, those questions are some I ask myself daily. If the same answer keeps coming up, then I know it's time to be brave and make a change.

Another self-test I use is related to ease. If things don't happen easily, I pause. If things feel like a struggle, I consider that as a red flag that I need to address before moving forward. This doesn't mean my chosen path will be without travail, hardship, and work. These are to be expected. But, when I look closely at a situation that doesn't feel easy, I try to discern whether things are hard because they are out of alignment, a boundary has been crossed, or if there is an essential lesson I need to learn from the situation at hand.

Questions I ask myself about ease include:

- *When do I find myself in a smooth flow of work, focus, or play?*
- *When do I feel out-of-sync or out of flow?*
- *Why is this value, habit, choice, or scenario so hard to live out?*

When we cannot come up with solutions on our own, we should ask our communities for assistance, especially our elders. We should prioritize this option over outsourcing our questions to people and objects with no real relation to ourselves. *Just ask Siri*, we often say. *Google it*, we tell each other. I'm not adverse to admitting that the internet and technology can give us information in split seconds, but are the answers they give in alignment with the same values you hold? Who then, do we seek counsel from? We must reestablish a norm of making time to be in community and receive advice from elders and wise people in our lives. And we must accept that doing so will take more time, energy, and discomfort than using technology or paying a quick fee. Of course, it can feel incredibly uncomfortable and vulnerable to ask someone in our circle about their life decisions, and in return, tell them about our own struggles. However, if we outsource our solutions to robots the advice we get is also manufactured and one-dimensional. If we connect to humans who have lived a rich life, we receive counsel that includes personal, historical wisdom from a lived experience.

Let's look deeper into the example of how I used my newly awoken intuition as director of our K-8 farm co-op program. During our third year of having the K-8 program, we operated on farmland which came with the responsibility of running a farm. This included taking care of goats and chickens as well as maintaining vegetables. Buying this land meant we had leveled up, but we soon realized we were in over our heads. I felt constricted regarding a lot of my new duties. This meant not being able to take any extended time away from Tacoma with my family. We value travel, and I wanted to spend time with our family in Guatemala for longer periods of time. So, I sat down and worked to dig up the roots of my discontent in this area of my life. This storyline was,

> *I have to work at the farm to make sure it doesn't get overtaken by weeds and so we don't waste any food. Farms should look clean, tidy, and well-maintained. It takes a full-time job to run a farm.*

I started to play around with different narratives I could use, or ways of thinking about my role on the farm and my relationship to the food I was producing through the co-op program. My goal was to find a narrative that released me from the "I have to…" mindset. I landed on one that resonated deeply with me, and which I am still using to this day.

> *I get to tend to the land through dreams it shares with me. I get to play at the farm, get my hands dirty and see the magic of new life sprouting. I get to fill my fridge with fresh eggs and produce that my kids helped plant, grow, and harvest.*

This narrative felt lighter, better, and more playful.

Another area that brought up fear within my mind and body was that of hard work during the summer months. As a guide and director, I wanted to be free to play, rest, and travel during the summer. As I sat with my fear of being confined to the farm, a dream started to grow inside me. It grew an exoskeleton, first, during a drive to Portland. Jose sat next to me and let me dream and ramble about possible farm solutions. I mentioned CSA boxes, and while I continued to talk, Jose researched the price of local CSA boxes and how much land leases for near our farm. The more we discussed and researched local CSA programs, the more the possibility of leasing our farm to farmers who would set up a CSA program seemed not only logical, but fruitful. My dream then developed scales and wings. In the car, we brainstormed who in our community might be interested in developing the CSA program on the land. In this version of my dream, my family could release ourselves from an unrealistic amount of land management; share the work of farming with our community and return to enjoying our time on the farm. We could also share the benefits of land stewardship with our marginalized communities. This dream was directly in line with my intuition, which was telling me that our current situation didn't match up with those values. We needed to realign ourselves to our beliefs surrounding land tending and redistribution of resources. My intuition was trying to show me that addressing this situation would also bring my family closer to returning to our ideal lifestyle. So, my work at that moment was to listen to my intuition, dream up possibilities in line with it, and connect to the wisdom of other farmers already involved in CSAs. I needed to find partners who would benefit and align with the opportunity, and together, we could put the plan into action.

It took us over a year to figure out how to bring this dream to fruition. Some of the work included working with organizations that connected farmers to land. Other work included partnering with a Kenyan farmer to grow produce as part of their own CSA program, which distributes food to immigrants who need it. We bartered office space in exchange for maintenance and fresh produce. We changed the way we ran the farm by incorporating automation, like automatic doors and water timers, which would allow the farm to be more self-sufficient and our family to recoup much of our time at home. We also adjusted our annual travel home to Guatemala to match the farm's natural cycles of growth and decay.

If there are areas of your life in which you feel stuck, like I was, know that there are better options calling for you in this world. There are more satisfying lifestyles. There are moral pathways more aligned with your values and desired state of being. The solutions are there, but we must slow down, sit still, listen deeply, and tune-in to ourselves to align with them. Only then can we feel our deep-rooted desires, share our truth, revise old habits, and build new and realized possibilities for ourselves.

It takes guts to do this work. Surely, you'll have to change old, ingrained habits and shed old narratives like clothing that no longer fits. Most likely, you'll have to adopt a countercultural lifestyle. But, once you take that first step, you will realize you aren't the only one doing so. There are many others on similar and parallel journeys to yours. Some are just planting the seeds of their dreams, some are transplanting the sprouts, and some are harvesting their dreams. The key is to disconnect from false rhythms, reconnect with your intuition and self-trust, listen to the voices deep inside you and the voices of those in your trusted circles.

Our family has been on our own path, toward a life more aligned with our values, for almost a decade. Our journey started on a drive to the Olympic peninsula, with our one-year-old in the back seat. I was radically honest with Jose about how little I enjoyed teaching in public schools. I admitted that my favorite part of work was conducting Friday Nature Explorations in which I took students outside to explore and discover what Nature offers. Ten years after that car drive, the results have been two outdoor educational programs, a connected community who celebrates together, and days spent outdoors teaching social justice. The fabric of those first dreams was woven into something magical. This magic is possible and available to you too. I promise you, your current places of constriction and frustration will alchemize into something new and sustainable if you let them. Begin by trusting your inner wisdom, turning to the wisdom in your community, sharing vulnerably, and daring to dream. Then see what takes flight.

Invitations for Reflection

Starting a nature school begins with an internal journey of reconnecting with your intuition. Grab a blank piece of paper and answer each of these questions for yourself before moving to the next chapter:

- In what areas of my life do I feel constriction?

- In what areas of my life do I feel flow, ease, and freedom?

- What is keeping me in the same stuck loop in this life?

- What is one part of my daily rhythm I want to reinvent and tweak?

- How do I feel about the holidays and traditions I celebrate?

- What other routines, traditions, and people deserve more of my time?

- Do I feel magic in my day? If so, where and how do I get more of that?

Consider taking the following actions:

- Find someone who has started a nature school or another business and ask to go and sit in their space for a few days while they work. Observe how they run their program and the nuts and bolts of how it works.

- Increase your time in silence. Start small with 10-20 minutes each day. Include silence in your other activities. For example, when washing the dishes, do so in silence. Gradually increase your silent time and notice if you can attune quicker to your inner voice.

- Welcome dreams by putting a journal next to your bed. When you have a dream, write it down. Ask for dreams before you go to sleep.

- Establish relationships with people who also listen to their intuition. Be brave and share with them how you've made decisions using your intuition. When they share about their life, ask them questions about their inner voice and heart-led decision making. Set goals together.

- Find intuitives in your community or world. Follow them, subscribe to their podcasts, and read their work. See who they follow and look into that media to see if they are your "flavor."

- Begin a morning or night-time ritual that includes silence, meditation, tarot cards, cold plunging, gratitude journaling, dancing, coloring, singing, rocking, humming, stretching or free-writing. Write down anything that pops into your mind when doing these rituals. Use your journals as a record and reminder of what Spirit is telling, teaching or guiding you to do.

- Pay attention to things that happen three times or more in your life. If the same message or guidance comes from three different sources, I perk up and pay attention, knowing something important is happening. This is something to add to your writing during journal and reflection time.

- Pay attention to emotions and honor them by naming them. This moves the emotion and prevents it from getting stuck. The more adept you are at naming emotions, the better you can identify and respond to them. A constant feeling of grumpiness around something is a signal telling you to take action or make a change in that area.

- Find and remain in a state of ease. Return to the questions earlier in the chapter that focus on cultivating ease.

The work of cultivating and trusting your intuition is never done. Revisit this step monthly, or as needed, while embarking on your journey to start a nature program.

Chapter 2
Reprioritize Holistic Wellness

Once we have built our inner intuition we start to see the world through different lenses. We began to see injustice and imbalance in our major systems of health and education. I never thought we would need to advocate for the basic wellness and needs of our children. Yet, there are advocacy groups such as National Association for the Education of Young Children and Institute of Play that fight for children's rights to play and whose sole purpose is to remind us of the power of play, for both children and adults. Who would have known that my childhood of blanket forts and mud kitchens would be a controversial topic for caregivers in modern times?

Children deserve outspoken advocates for wellness and balance in their childhoods. What I am referring to when I say "wellness and balance" is a state in which a child's natural inclinations are honored and prioritized over things imposed on them from outside sources. Natural inclinations include the inclination to play, to feel safe, to eat whole foods, to enter flow, to move slowly, to be curious, or to move our bodies. Things imposed on them might include the introduction of screen time at a young age, inappropriately early academics, scary and/or violent content, being still or inside all day, or consuming highly processed foods. Don't get me wrong, no one can be well and balanced all the time, but that doesn't disqualify us and shouldn't discourage us from attempting to offer that to our children.

Let's look more closely at how wellness and balance play out with an example regarding academics. Our current culture praises and encourages high academic achievements, which sometimes results in parents feeling pressured to introduce academics to their children too early in their young lives. School districts have consistently pushed down standards which were originally created for higher grades and are now expectations geared towards kindergarteners and first graders. I watch parents feel pride in introducing early academics into their children's lives. And why wouldn't they? We feel proud when our children show signs of wanting to read at age three. It's brag-worthy, for sure. But we quickly forget children need to learn through their hands, that using a worksheet isn't the best way for little fingers to learn letters. A child's gift is to see wonder, to move slowly, to get down in the dirt and explore. Children do not have the same rhythm or ambitions as adults, nor should they. So why do we try to impart early academics, through worksheets, screens, or apps, onto our children at a young age? Early academic achievement is a value of our society, but it doesn't have to be a value of our families. Families can choose to say, "Thank you, but no thank you."

I am deeply passionate about a balanced and healthy childhood for all children. Nowadays, this is labeled an alternative or countercultural parenting philosophy. Whatever we call it, the philosophy focuses on the power of play for children of preschool and early education age. It gives young children opportunities for dress up, tea parties, and mud play, rather than worksheets or memorization. NIFP and Dr. Brown define the word "play" as an activity that includes all of <u>Dr. Peter Gray's</u> five elements of play. According to Dr. Gray, play is:

1. Self-chosen and self-directed.
2. Intrinsically motivated.
3. Structured or ordered based on rules in the player's mind.
4. Imaginative, or has a creative aspect.
5. A playful state of mind—the player is very engaged, alert, mentally active, and focused on the activity, but is not stressed about the activity (they have no fear of judgment, and there are no consequences that matter outside of the activity itself) (2013, p.140).

Play is the best way to learn. I trust that play is enough. I have faith that our children will be ready for academics when they are older but do not need to be stressed out by it at a young age. Play builds a strong foundation for children and is the essential need for a well-balanced and nourished child. Offering ample opportunities for play and unstructured time results in children who are connected to their emotions, know how to communicate their needs, are aware of what they like and dislike, can mend and repair after conflict, are creative and imaginative, and value the need for fun. A deficiency in play can lead to depression, lack of empathy, poor impulse control, and mood-driven behaviors. According to the National Institute of Play (The Basics, n.d.), "Research into human play is growing across many scientific disciplines (para 1). Neuroscientists have shown that play circuits are pre-wired in our brains at birth. Evolutionary biologists have shown that play behaviors have evolved over eons to enhance our adaptability and thus our survival. Education researchers have shown that playing equals learning." So put away those worksheets and learning apps and get outside where the invitations to play and learn are endless.

Teach Beyond Academics

So, what should the younger members of society, between the ages of two and five years old, be doing instead of learning to recite words or answering math equations? My resounding answer would be moral intelligence and social aptitude learned through play with peers and whole-body involvement. For our children ages six and up, we can focus on academics, while integrating play and movement into every lesson. Maria Montessori has said, "What the hand does, the mind remembers (Maunz, 2022)."

At Chavitos, we know there is more to life than just academic intelligence. We devote time to the 10 Intelligences, taught by Howard Gardner. They are spatial, body-kinesthetic, emotional, musical, naturalistic, interpersonal, creative, intrapersonal, existential, and collaborative skills. The soft skills of self-awareness, moral intelligence, tolerance of others, acceptance, and external awareness through conversation, modeling behavior, and adjusting expectations are essential for success, health, connection, and overall happiness (Gardner, 2011).

With preschool students, we focus on play as the primary vehicle for cultivating a child's social-emotional and relational development. Being around other children naturally allows them access to real opportunities for learning and practicing lessons. When a child wants to swing, but the swing is in use by another child, we see the situation as an invitation for the child waiting for the swing to practice patience, to communicate their wants, and to identify and dive into any feelings arising from the situation. This is also an opportunity to practice empathy towards other children.

Presenting these concepts to elementary children looks similar. We teach them to eat when they are hungry instead of waiting for an official snack time. We encourage children to take work breaks, find a cozy spot, or find safe ways to meet their sensory input needs away from activity or stimuli. We replace walking in lines or sitting for an hour of lecture with natural movement and intuitive learning. There are multiple seating options, like wobbly logs or pillows, and spaces to meet the varying needs of the children. Pillows, hammocks, ear protection and a wide range of materials are available and can be accessed at any time throughout the day. We teach all children to advocate for themselves when they need space to process emotions or need support from a guide.

With elementary and middle school students, we dive into academics while still including and encouraging movement, cultivating curiosity, and using hands-on application of learning components. Woven in every interaction is teaching the students how to listen to their needs, identify and voice what they need, and make requests to their guides. We interweave these learning points into fun, engaging lessons that include a lot of play.

For all humans, both young and old, we believe play is the perfect conduit to naturally build and practice essential social-emotional and relational skills. Wellness for children means advocating for unstructured play, creating environments of wonder, and inviting them to dive into their imagination. When a child's whole body is engaged in the learning process, we find they are better able to dive into emotional and educational explorations. Simply put, children learn best through play and movement. Caregivers can offer opportunities for play and movement by sampling activities from the list below.

Play in the Chavitos Forest with preschoolers includes:

- Running back and forth through long wooded areas
- Taking an "independent" hike through the forest
- Digging and building in the sand pit with molds and shovels, and adorning with pinecones, rocks, or leaves
- Creating a mud pie in the kitchen and serving it to a friend

- Filling and pulling a wagon through skinny forest trails
- Stacking tires and filling them with wood chips
- Collecting flower petals and crushing them to make a potion
- Swinging
- Climbing trees and hanging from branches
- Lining up pinecones in a pattern
- Harvesting and eating seasonal fruit
- Drawing, grinding and painting with chalk
- Play we witness with K-8 students includes:
- Digging tunnels through the center of a fresh wood chip pile
- Splashing through rain puddles
- Pretending to be animals and prey
- Creating a cleaning station business when gear gets muddy
- Using pipe cleaners and buttons to create wearable jewelry
- Using imagination to organize and leadership to direct an impromptu fashion show or circus
- Folding paper airplanes and seeing how far they go
- Hiding under cedar trees when playing a game
- Brushing, holding and harvesting garden snippets for guinea pigs
- Harvesting kale and leaves for hungry grateful goats
- Walking goats on a leash or harness to a fresh patch of food
- Rock hunting and identifying gems
- Creating obstacle courses through mud puddles with boards and found materials
- Rocking each other on the hammock, which might have been transformed into a spaceship
- Creating a restaurant in the mud kitchen with elaborate roles inspired by Gordon Ramsey
- Balancing on logs and moving others to create ramps

- Harvesting mint and herbs for tea
- Following and observing our chicken flock

There are lessons infused into various kinds of play. Here are some examples of how play offers learning opportunities to children in both our programs, regardless of age.

- A child fills up water containers until the water overflows. *The child learns about volume and capacity.*
- A child is accidentally knocked down by a friend on the swing. *The child learns about force and gravity. Things are pulled to the ground.*
- A child singing on the stage is interrupted by a friend. *The child learns how to set boundaries, share their feelings about what they don't like, and verbally express their needs.*
- A child is pecked by a chicken when they are holding it tightly to their body. *The child learns how animals communicate their needs.*
- A child goes to fill their water bucket, but the rain barrel is empty. *The child learns water is life and a finite resource.*
- A child is pulled in the wagon and starts crying before the wagon tips over. *The child learns to make clear requests when something is "too much" for them.*
- A child breaks a window on the greenhouse by carrying a big stick in a small space. *The child learns spatial awareness and the effect their actions have on the environment around them.*
- A child pees their pants and hides. A guide supports them to come out of hiding and gets them into clean, dry clothes. *The child learns we can always show up for each other and we don't need to hide our mistakes from others. There is always support around us and we can ask for help when we need it.*

- A child requests a class meeting to openly discuss a problem they have with another child. *The child learns how to advocate for their needs, engage in healthy conflict, compromise, and repair after conflict.*
- A child drops their snack on the floor. Another child offers to share their snack with them. *Both children learn that problems can be solved with community support.*
- A guide quits and moves on to another job. *Children learn that relationships are fluid. Change is inevitable. We can continue to connect in different ways and it's okay to miss and love someone.*

One of the perks of my job as director of educational programs is deciding where to focus our programs. In our K-8 program, I pause any lesson at any time to make space for the children's emotional well-being. This sometimes grinds on my teaching flow and shows up in my own colonized-school mindset (this is also the same mindset that was programmed into those of us who have been in formal education from preschool onward. It's the mindset that says, "Watch the clock! Get the lesson in! Increase the amount of information input! Forge forward to meet the goal! Improve test results."). As a certified teacher and product of America's educational system, this drive to "achieve" and "complete" is firmly programmed into most of us and it takes a real consciousness and awareness to unravel its entanglement.

When I started our nature programs nine years ago, I started a slow healing process from this mindset. Over time, it has become abundantly clear to me that when I take the time to pivot away from the day's lesson to meet the emotional needs of a child, the day goes better, not only for that individual child, but for the community as a whole. It feels better in everyone's hearts. This adjusted flow of teaching and honoring supports our program's values. Here's another example of how this plays out in real time during teaching:

CASE STUDY

I'm teaching a social justice lesson to our K-8 students. I'm in my flow, talking about food access, answering questions about what protesting is, and explaining who the Indigenous activist, Autumn Peltier is. While I'm talking, I see a little hand signing, "I'm hungry" in American Sign Language. To the left, I see another little hand signing to me, saying, "I need to use the bathroom!"

Internally, I feel annoyance rise up inside me. If they could just sit still and listen for five more minutes, I could wrap this lesson up and we could move forward as a group. I notice I'm now holding my breath. My tension builds.

I release my breath. I exhale deeply, trying to slow myself down. Then, I nod my head at both students trying to get my attention, letting them know I see them. I pause the lesson and check in with the rest of the group. I give them a choice of how we can proceed or include an impromptu partner share. I make adjustments as needed.

I acknowledge (to myself) that I want to keep going with our lesson. Then I remind myself that this — pausing to honor the children's bodies — is a supportive move. And it's the move that aligns with the educational model I want to cultivate, not just preach.

This demonstrates to the children that if they
share their needs and use their voices, others will listen to
their wants and needs. This represents the aligned move.
Validating their needs is critical to their long-term wellness.
By doing so, we're teaching them to listen to their natural
rhythms and honor what their bodies need, recognizing that
this is a model for others in their community to validate
their own requests.

I'm still in the process of letting my annoyance
move through me. Interrupting my lesson is a small hitch
in my plan, but it's more important to honor students'
needs. Doing so aligns with wellness and the overall well-
being of children.

Minutes later, those students have returned silently
to the lesson and other peers help them catch up. The
transition is quick. They now attend more attentively, since
they aren't feeling the pricks of hunger or the distraction
of a full bladder. Class runs seamlessly for the remainder of
our time together.

I wish all our lessons shook out as smoothly as this one. The
truth is, sometimes these transitions in and out of lessons can be messy and
distracting. But that's also where we collectively learn about acceptance,
reteaching boundaries, adjusting our expectations, and sharing the impact of
one's actions with vulnerability.

At preschool, we allow the rhythms of our bodies and the earth to
guide all instruction. We structure children's time at the preschool as "free

flow" because we deeply value the lessons and learning opportunities that arise organically when we pay attention to those rhythms and allow for play to naturally evolve out of them. When small children are afforded opportunities to choose how they want to play and who they want to play with, they grow their executive function to make choices. For this age group, we don't offer formal academics, circle times or planned reading aloud. We let the children romp and roll through the raspberry patches and dirt, instead. We let the winter weather, the warming fire, the chorus of birds, be their guides and inspiration.

Nature is the best teacher of "balance" because she models it. She teaches us that everything is connected, including the small bodies that play under her canopy. The children in the preschool forest learn about the life happening around them and overhead when they lay down to rest. They learn about the other beings they share the forest with, such as when a scrub jay comes to clean up their snack crumbs. They learn a shovel in use by another student is not available, but it will be soon. They learn patience when they hide behind a tree in a suspenseful game of hide and seek. They learn how to pivot and adjust when the rain comes and washes away their chalk art.

Similar to Nature, Chavitos instructors act as guides to the children. They're available to lead children in these experiences with nature and help model sharing feelings and setting boundaries with others. And, ultimately, our guides are there to teach children how to honor their wonder, value their creativity, explore their edges, and engage with their big emotions. Wellness for children comes from connecting them to powers and entities bigger than themselves and then letting them investigate and discover mysteries according to their own timing and rhythms (which is often significantly slower than that of adults and older children).

Relational Wellness

All humans are connected to other humans and beings. For most of us it's very rare to be hermits and in continual states of solitude. So, it's essential we learn how to be in relationship with others. Adults know that our friendships and connections are constantly changing. We might know what type of people we enjoy being around the most or which type of personality makes us shut down in annoyance. It takes a long time to learn about ourselves and other personalities. Gardener (2011) describes this as interpersonal intelligence or knowing how to read and interact with other people. Just like all other intelligences, children are born with a varying degree of skill sets and an innate ability to gauge interactions with others. Even so, all people need to see this modeled and continue practicing interpersonal skills. At Chavitos, our philosophy is to make time to learn and practice skills such as empathy, sharing, cooperation, listening, following directions, respecting personal space, making eye contact, and using manners.

One way we can be in relationship with each other is by sharing emotions that happen during shared events. For example, grief, when experienced alone, can be isolating and disorientating. It can be consuming and bleed into all other areas of our lives. When my dad died, I realized Americans didn't have very helpful or supportive systems for grief. Recently, *Yes Magazine* published an article titled "The Revolutionary Power of Grieving in Public" by Yolande Clark-Jackson (2024). In it, she states,

> *"There's evidence that supports that sharing the burden of grief in public invites others to aid in the healing process. It can also allow a stronger social resilience to discuss topics of grief and mourning. And it connects us to community in ways that may be able to enact change. In short, externalization and communal*

care of grief can be transformative" (para.2).

CASE STUDY

Our K-8 students got to experience this connection with grief a few times in 2023. One such example was when one of our guides quit suddenly and unexpectedly. The immediacy of their decision gave their fellow guides and students no notice or information surrounding their departure. It seemed that most of the students' grief was felt around not being able to say goodbye. Our guides saw the importance of creating space for grief and reflection, so we reorganized our lesson plans and gathered in a circle to process and share what was happening. Taking time to listen and share openly lets the students express their loss, transition, and confusion with each other. Ultimately, doing so allowed them to move their pain from their bodies so it wouldn't result in paralysis, sickness, or distress. We all need more compassionate spaces where we can connect, receive validation and have an opportunity to be cared for by others. Having those spaces and opportunities normalizes the feeling of grief and how it shows up in our bodies as stress, worry, or anger. My hope is that when they become adults, Chavitos students will continue to create these spaces in their homes, friendships, and professions.

When we create spaces to unite over shared beliefs, the results are that we become more unified and in closer relationship with others. Clark-Jackson (2024) writes, "We've seen environmental activism as the result of the grief over environmental degradation. We've seen the women's rights movement come as a result of the grief over gender inequality, and global movements for justice following the grief over political or racial injustice" (para 5). I've seen our strong, resilient, heart-led group of children learn to hold space for peers and their adults. I believe they will become leaders who emphasize the importance of being in close relation with others. They will be creators of spaces that center authentic relationships. We do this work not because it's easy, but because it's important and essential. I want a generation that prioritizes relationships first over production, tasks, and accomplishments. With connection at the center of our values, we are redesigning the hierarchy of needs, making it less about individualism and more about interdependence. This shift has the power to change all types of leadership, and hopefully, larger social systems.

All relationship skills need to be modeled, taught, and expected. At Chavitos you will see guides pausing a lesson for an impromptu class meeting. Or, rescheduling our day to include conversations about an impactful event that happened while we were together. In the forest, a guide will gather students playing roughly and guide them with questions like,

> *How do you feel?*
> *How do you think your friend feels?*
> *What do you need?*

I also expect our guides to model working through relational issues verbally with each other in front of children. Young ones need to witness adults in conflict, adults mending, and adults moving forward in health.

One of our best tools for this is a simple routine with a blank notebook. We title the notebook, "Classroom Problem Solving Notebook." It is a simple tool that can be replicated in any setting. Our notebook is kept in a central and agreed upon location. Inside the lined pages, students write down a problem they are having or observed from others at Chavitos. When done, they let a guide know they have a problem, and together, they find a time to hold a class meeting. During a class meeting, we gather in a circle. The person who wrote the problem leads the meeting. We honor talking openly to each other, using each other's names, adding specifics to support our observations, and always including "I feel" statements of how the situation made us feel so we can inspire empathy and soften our sharing (so it isn't received as an accusation). Next, we turn to the brain power of the collective. All the students can brainstorm possible solutions. All ideas are written down and honored. Sometimes a guide might need to clarify to best understand how one idea was different from another. The final step is to vote. Everyone votes on which solution we would like to try. If this problem was a result of one person's choices, we also take time to build that student up and refill their love tank by sharing what we love about them. We end with chants of "We love you!" We intentionally want students to be held accountable for their choices and know we all make mistakes and have the power to change our choices if we are hurting others. We never force an apology and always allow time to hear both sides of the story, knowing it's important to have a full view of a situation when mending and problem solving.

Our ritual of class meetings works because our community of guides and students holds common values. Some of the principles we hold in circle include:

- Clear is kind (Brown, 2018).

- We share without blame.

- We practice active listening and give signals that we hear what the speaker is saying (by practicing nodding our heads and repeating back what we hear).

- We accept feedback.

- We don't make excuses. We take responsibility for our choices. We acknowledge how our choices have hurt another.

- We solve problems by looking at all solutions before choosing one to move forward with. We think-up wild and out of the box ideas. We even entertain silly and whimsical ideas to make the process fun and lighter.

- We end our time in circle with love. We check in with those involved and make sure they are feeling heard and seen. We chant "We love you" or "We declare peace!" These declarations unify us and remind us we are fully supportive of each other.

After we end our time in a circle, we slip seamlessly back into our regularly scheduled lessons with calm bodies and peaceful minds. Because we've addressed issues at hand, the children are often able to focus better, and the lesson is received because their minds and bodies were tended to. I often do my best teaching after circle because I'm fueled by the hope that the children gathered around me are learning these important interpersonal skills that will make our world a more peaceful place. These children are our future, and we need a future full of people who are well and balanced.

Wellness for our future and the world starts in nature, with children playing in the forest and problem solving over mud kitchen potions. Well children turn into well adults who turn into well leaders. In turn, that wellness transforms our surroundings into a healthy world.

Invitations for Reflection

- Do I have healthy and helpful ways to express all my emotions?

- Which of the 10 intelligences, taught by Howard Gardner, do I embody and utilize? Which intelligences do I want to grow in? How can I improve my relationship with them?

- What types of play did I enjoy the most as a child? Do I still get enjoyment from these activities?

- Where can I create invitations for others to play?

- How do I hold space for others? What areas can I grow in to become a better caregiver?

Consider taking the following actions:

- Plan rituals and routines that support and hold space for emotions and problem solving.

- Find models and rituals that already exist. Adjust them to make them your own.

- Find and use accurate language regarding your own feelings. This way you can model to your students how to articulate and share honestly. A feelings thesaurus is a useful tool for this.

Chapter 3
Realign Routines & Values

In 2001, I traveled to Kipkaren, Kenya, to work in a children's home as part of Empowering Lives International. One of my nightly rhythms was visiting the kids in their shared rooms. I would tuck the checkered bed sheets under each of their brilliant, smiling faces, saying goodnight to all twenty-four of them. Afterwards, I would relax with their home parents. We would sit in their living room with cups of sweet chai steaming on the coffee table, and swap cultural and life stories. One of our first conversations was about me, and how I had gotten to Kenya. I was twenty-four years old, and I was proud to have traveled many airplane miles and multiple connections myself. The parents were astonished, but not for the reasons I expected.

"What-O! You came by yourself? Next time bring some others."

With this unexpected yet simple response, my American mantle of individualism had its first crack on its once pristine surface. *What? These friends didn't value independence and self-sufficiency? What did they value instead?* What a wakeup call! I realized my idea of moving through the world wasn't the only option for doing so. And maybe it wasn't the best

either. From a young age, American culture had instilled a sense of pride
in me about being independent, accomplishing success on my own, and
not needing support or help from others. But other cultures aren't fed this
same dogma. From a young age, people in other cultures learn the power
of community, the reality that we are stronger together, and the wisdom
that we need each other to thrive. My experiences in Kenya helped me shift
and challenge the values and beliefs of my culture, and what it means to
stand in community.

We need to clearly understand what our values are in life. Then,
we can use our values to redefine what success means to us. Often, we're
encouraged to be independent, and that independence is better than being
part of a collective. But that's a social construct which leads to loneliness
and burnout. Our children, ourselves as caregivers, and our communities are
all positioned within larger networks of mutual care. We need to return to a
way of living that is structured around collectives rather than individuals. To
do so, we first need to build awareness of the stories we're telling children at
a young age. We are asked, *What do you want to be when you grow up?* Or we
put our children into boxes by saying things like, *When you are married, and
you have children…*

Our social conditioning goes much deeper than we like to admit.
But when we pay attention to commercials or listen to ads on the radio or
tv, we can clearly see the life we are being sold. When we read children's
books, we see what kind of life is represented as "typical," with the
assumption that readers want the same for their families. But what if we
decided not to allow ourselves to be so influenced, and instead, tune into
our aspirations for how we want to structure our family lives?

When I was pregnant with my first child, I taught at a public
Montessori school. I enjoyed many aspects of my work, but I had a growing
dissatisfaction with the structures and storylines there. One day, I was sitting

at a whole school assembly with the kids in my class, seated criss-cross on the freshly mopped tiled floor, while teachers and guests sat in metal folding chairs to the side. My friend Andee said, "Pretty soon, your Keats will be sitting here with us." While this was intended as a simple statement of connection, it rattled me and woke me up. *Was this what I wanted my own son's school experience to be like?* There was something about the cold floor, the lines of students waiting to sit down, and the sterileness of the school, overall, that rubbed me the wrong way. I didn't like the expectation that over 100 students should sit still and quietly wait for all the classes to arrive and for the event to start. This expectation didn't sit well with me. I realized this educational model didn't align with my family's values. I thought maybe I could offer a different experience to my child.

So, I did things differently. My husband and I sat down and made a list of what we wanted for our child's education, as opposed to what was currently offered. After my first child was born, I returned to work and my husband stayed home with them. While I taught, Jose parented. At twenty-eight years old, Jose had just immigrated from Guatemala and was learning English and the routines of a stay-at-home parent and American culture. This arrangement worked for us. My child was immersed in Spanish and Jose learned English at Play to Learn programming in our city. Jose and our son got to explore public transportation, our neighborhood, and parks. I remember coming home one day to Jose sitting in our recliner in a cloud of clean cloth diapers. As he folded them, my son slept, mouth wide open in Jose's arms. I loved seeing how involved Jose was with our son, especially since he grew up in a machismo culture where dad's roles were hands off from kid duties and home responsibilities. Here, Jose was kind and involved, helping our household run smoothly and fulfilling roles in the family that his culture would have scoffed at. At the time, due to my work demands, Jose started to cook meals at home. He didn't have a driver's license, or speak or read English at the time, so I did the meal planning. Grocery shopping was a weekly family event. We dealt-out family roles according to our capabilities and availability. Luckily, neither he nor I thought twice about this. The arrangement fit my rebel personality. And, truth be told, having met in Guatemala on a service trip with the non-profit, Camino Seguro, we never were conventional in the roles within our personal relationship.

Unsurprisingly, when our first child was still a baby, we started to dream of different opportunities for him, too. What if my child didn't have to spend time in a hyper-controlled school where children walk in lines, go to the bathroom at designated times, or sit in over-crowded classrooms? What if he wanted to run or skip to class? What if he wanted to talk and process experiences with his friends in the hallways? What if he wanted to continue his conversation with his friend as they went to get their lunch? What if he had more than thirty sacred minutes of recess each day? What if he could move during his whole school day as his body needed? What if he could still speak Spanish, his primary language? I began to deep-dive into reimagining what my son's childhood could look like as well as what my life as a teacher could look like.

What if I took the parts of education I loved most and made those the norm instead of the exception?

This question is just one example of giving ourselves permission to challenge the cultural narrative of how we should function as parents, or what schooling for our children should look like. For our family, these two structures are deeply intertwined. To restructure our family dynamics, we had to find an educational system that would fit our needs. Since that didn't exist yet, we had to dream of a new educational model to offer to our children, and other children, in our city. We had to give ourselves permission to dream. I still wrestle with this — giving myself permission to dream, to defy societal norms about family life — daily. My doubt whispers,

Are you giving your children enough quality time during the week?

Are we, as parents, protecting them too much? My now eleven-year-old son brings his stuffed animal into the grocery store and loves to cuddle...

Shouldn't your multiracial kids be around more children who look like them?

When I dig for the answers to these questions within myself, I realize my parenting style is counterculture to standard expectations. And I don't mind that. I like the way our family rolls. I like the way I show up as a mom. I like the agreements my family has made so far, and I'm grateful we continue to question our agreements as we grow. Here are some of our current family agreements and rhythms, which I hope can serve as inspirational examples to other caregivers who seek to engage in non-dominant cultural practices of their own:

- The kids wake up early before Jose and I. They usually read books and cuddle on the couch. Jose and I keep sleeping even after the kids wake up. If hungry, they have direct access to healthy foods.

- We live with a "bonus family," or another family living in the finished downstairs apartment within our home. We might hear a knock at the basement door and open it to find a little brown face with loving eyes greeting us, holding a container of beans their parent cooked and wanted to share, or simply saying, *Goodnight.*

- We take weekly trips to the library. Our kids gather books to return, and we always bring new books home with us. We make time for this tradition because we value and love reading together. The library is a free resource and expands our minds.

- We are one-car puzzling ninjas! We intentionally have one car and so we stack our activities (and make the most use of our time). If we go out, we try to go to multiple places in one trip. We carpool with friends to bigger events and try to find stores close to our home to shop at. This takes flexibility and spaciousness, but that's not a problem because we have space in our schedule to accommodate changes. Sometimes I text Jose to pick up our bulk food order on his way home from getting the oil changed. Or, better yet, we ask friends in our community who might already be out and about to pick up our order when they pick up theirs.

- We teach door-knocking and value time alone. From a very young age, we teach our kids that a closed door needs to be knocked on, not simply opened. If we don't answer, then they know whoever is on the other side isn't available. This is a great lesson for our kids, as it models several things at once. If I don't answer my bedroom door, I am communicating not only my special boundary, but my need to end my day early, read a book in bed, and prioritize my rest. Of course, this requires preparation. As a family, we make sure to leave healthy and appropriate snacks accessible to our kids. And we've taught independence enough for our children to access what they need. This means there is a stool our seven-year-old can easily access and maneuver to reach the cups and plates.

- We celebrate how and what we want to celebrate. If a celebration becomes a burden, we revisit it and realign. We've made yearly traditions of visiting our favorite hot springs in Breitenbush in

Detroit, Oregon. We buy an experience, instead of an object, as a gift when celebrating the winter solstice. We have an altar prominent in our home that keeps us connected to our ancestors daily. We eat tamales at Christmas. We don't celebrate Mother's Day, Father's Day, or Valentine's Day. Instead, we save that money for our international trips.

- We live by the cycles of the earth we tend. We celebrate those cycles by eating seasonal foods at biweekly dinners with friends. We try to buy local food from farmers markets and grow our own food.

- We only have Friday movie nights in winter. We have clear boundaries around screen time.

- We organize sleepovers with our community so Jose and I can go on a date and connect without interruptions. We know it's important we continue to like each other, and having fun together just the two of us reminds us why we fell in love. Our children spend that time at a friend's house, and later in the month, those friends will come to our house for a sleepover. We all save money and invest in each other.

- We are intentional with how we spend our money and focus that spending in places that support people who we want to see prosper. Our spending is aligned to our values of travel, culture, and supporting local, BIPOC and LGBTQ+ small businesses.

- We are intentional about how we save by waiting to buy what we need on sale, buying used and repurposed, and fixing things that break in our home. We buy in bulk from organizations like Azure

Standard. We mostly cook at home. We have a budget for eating out. We use food as medicine as a preventive health measure.

Each family's agreements will look different, and each season will bring potential changes to those agreements. As our kids age, our needs as parents will change, too. And the community we engage with moves on sometimes, too. The important thing to remember is to live life in ways that nourish your family. Realign to your family's values, not those you're told to follow, and spend time doing the things that support those values.

Living a family life where every member uses their gifts and capacities was not something modeled to me when growing up. I didn't see anything like this. Now, I understand that this is okay. Maybe what we did at the time did, in fact, work for my parents. Maybe it didn't. The important thing here is noticing. I try to notice which rituals and routines my family holds that can also be a measuring stick for analysis as we (re)shape our own rhythms. For example, one thing I've always wanted more of is community. In Guatemala, I see firsthand how living in close community with family and friends can offer that. Guatemalan ways of living in community have become a goal for me. In Guatemala, a lot of my family lives together. My children's grandparents live in the same house or down the road, aunts and uncles flow freely in and out of the house, and cousins gather and play together. This multigenerational living is beneficial to everyone: the elders who soak up the energy and joy of children, the child who gains wisdom and lessons from crones, and the parents who receive extra support and connection from other adults in the vicinity.

Most cultures have alloparents, as well. But, not in the U.S. Still, I have always known I wanted this for my family. For many years I dreamed of living in a commune, and I still desire my grown children to live on shared land with Jose and me. I don't want to rely solely on my husband or the occasional support from parents living in another state or in different countries. So, I do my part to offer my children opportunities to develop deep, nourishing relationships with trusted adults in my community. We call them our chosen family.

If you have yet to find your community, look for people, organizations, and places where you see the values you hold or desire in life. Then reach for them. Most likely, there is a group of people in the world who speak your language. Following your bliss will lead you to them. I've found community in my herbal apprenticeship at Hawthorn and Honey. It is no accident that our nature programs are full of like-minded families who have been through similar processes of personal evaluation, reimagining, and realignment. Time and time again, I hear how at-peace families are with dropping their child off at the forest or farm where we caretake children, knowing this is how they have envisioned education and care at their best. They are in full alignment and trust regarding what will occur during school hours. They look forward to hearing the flood of stories at pick-up, and witnessing their child grow.

And remember, all of this is a *process*. Building community and realigning your routines and habits to your values takes time, intention, and a lot of effort. Our family and the Chavitos community is always growing, and everyone involved continues to work hard at being honest about their wants and needs, pruning what doesn't work for them.

Invitations for Reflection

- Make a list of your family routines. How do these routines feel for you? How do they feel for various family members? If needed, have a family meeting to find out about others' ideas. What routines does your family want to keep? Which ones have they outgrown?

- Is there anything your family has mastered within your routines? Write them down to celebrate them, and to notice any patterns among them.

- What parts of your routine feel challenging? How can you make a small change to this area of your life?

- What changes would you make to routines that feel uncomfortable? Make a list of ideas. Choose one idea and act upon it.

Give yourself permission to find sustainable rhythms that meet your particular familial needs and give each other permission to admit what isn't working, celebrating what is.

Chapter 4
Chavitos Values

When Jose and I created Chavitos, I knew I wanted to be part of something bigger than my tiny family of four. I wanted a life of real community and interwoven friendships, a web of connection that was strong enough for those within to hold each other during the high winds and battering rains of life. We wanted our children to remain at the center of our community. With this mission as our foundation, we began to build a business. We started with a partnership of land use with a family who knew us from my time teaching at Geiger. We held work parties to prepare the forest for our program. We made potlucks a monthly event and we bartered with friends so they could afford to send their children to our program. We were also honest with people about our goal of having a diverse group of children and guides within the program. We saw our light attract and draw others who were seeking much of the same.

An unexpected perk was that our son's friends from Chavitos preschool became friends with us outside that environment. And then they, and their families, became our family friends. For the first time in our lives, it was like our family wasn't speaking gibberish or feeling like square pegs in round holes. We were spending our time with other parents and families who had the same values as those we demonstrated in our business. The friendships were organic and grew in the nourishing soil of our clear and specific values. Naturally, through monthly forest potlucks, work parties hefting wood chips, and marimba concerts, we created deep, meaningful connections. We used our values to build a business, which, in turn, created a connective community. We'll examine those Chavitos values closely in this chapter, and hopefully, by the end of the chapter, you will be able to identify the values that will inspire your business and inevitably, your family.

Chavitos Values

Authenticity

We must allow ourselves and others to show up exactly as we are. As leaders, we strive to model this. If we believe all emotions are welcome, then we must show up grumpy, sad, angry, frustrated, at ease, etc. Kids can see through any pretending. We strive to be more authentic. The more real we are, the more we give others around us permission to fully show up as they are.

Being insincere or false takes energy to maintain. It can also be a safety mechanism for keeping people at a distance, or not facing some past trauma or deep, hidden pain. It can cause a lot of confusion and lead to disconnection. When we aren't genuine, we can't manifest our dreams because they aren't ours to begin with. They belong to another self, not our genuine self. But, when we show up as ourselves, we feel alive, connected to purpose, and connected to the bigger meaning of life. Loving ourselves and being open and real about our giftings and our struggles makes it easier to say yes or no to requests.

CASE STUDY

Last year, our K-8 community went through an upheaval. In the small neighborhood where our co-op was located, there was a single easement road leading to our farm. There were a few neighbors who didn't like the traffic, noise, or change we brought to the area. We had been fighting with them for two years, across multiple fronts, facing physical intimidation, reporting of our co-op to government and city organizations, disruption during the permitting process, and eventually, legal action against our co-op. We faced a deluge of attacks that made me bone tired.

When all this fighting began, I had tried the familiar approach of keeping my decision-making and problem-solving processes separate from my guides and families. I thought the process too messy, too worrisome, and too unstable to include our community in. The parents and guides trusted me to keep the program running, keep our kids safe, and provide their tuition's worth of education. But keeping everything to myself made me weary, isolated, and resulted in giving me major decision fatigue.

The second year, I realized my level of fatigue and decided to try a different approach to leadership, one I'd not witnessed or experienced yet. I wanted to share the burden, keep everyone informed, and be transparent in the process.

This new level of authenticity immediately felt more comfortable, but I was still worried about others' opinions and responses. The feedback has been both supportive and positive, and it resulted in a beautiful deepening and maturing of connection between myself and other parents in our community.

Eventually, we decided as a community to move our co-op program to a new location, Blue Heron Acres. We were tired of the daily harassment, and of the growing fear for the safety of our children and guides. During the decision-making process, my intention was to be real and transparent with parents, and that meant sharing these processes with them. I tried offering a new level of authenticity, where I shared snippets of my spiritual process with parents. I shared how I made decisions by first noticing how the proposed idea felt within my body. Goosebumps meant an idea that leaves me inspired, alive, and possible. This is a green light for me to move forward. Feelings of heaviness, weightiness, being stuck, or congestion mean I should dismiss the idea or try to reconfigure a new solution. This looks like changing different parts of the plan until it all feels good.

I shared this method in an email with families as we tried to decide where to move the co-op. I didn't want to hit send on that email! I felt embarrassingly "woo-woo," too spiritual and not logical enough for a business owner. I was worried my tactics would be interpreted as unprofessional. But I hit send anyway. Later that week, I chatted with one of our guides, Chris, who is also our van driver, a parent of two students, and the designer of our t-shirts and of this book cover. Chris commented on how my email had deeply encouraged him. He realized that he too makes decisions that way. It validated him. As we chatted about this, we watched the kids play mud ball soccer. His words were like a reward for the vulnerability I had shared. The wider fruits of this level of transparency have been incredible: reassurance that spirit and knowledge can lead a business, invitations for continued vulnerability, and ultimately, a deepening of connection and belonging. When doubting or wanting to shrink and show up partially, I'm reminded of how Chris is also making his own choices and decisions using the same method. When others see us showing up genuinely, it sets the expectation for everyone else to do the same. Being genuine gives each other permission to shine and be passionate about what makes them happy, not about what is most popular in the fleeting moment. Do you think this value of authenticity will be one of the cornerstones of your program?

Accessibility

Everyone who wants access to an alternative education should be able to have it. We attempt to increase the accessibility of our programs through three main systems:

1. Tuition support via barters and scholarships
2. Ensuring we have a diverse population of children in attendance
3. Using waitlists and enrollment policies to support the above systems

Barters are magical. They align with our values of equity in accessing quality childcare, and allow us to celebrate others' remarkable skills, training, and wisdom. In barters, we use a different type of wealth, one that exists outside capitalism. Barters offer a win-win scenario because both parties involved can give from a place of abundance. I have an abundance of teaching skills and therefore I can exchange those skills with someone who has skills I need but lack.

I've noticed when money is exchanged for services, it often occurs as a one-time, quick exchange. I'm grateful for those families who pay with money so we can pay our guides and mortgages. But the moment the money enters my accounts the interaction is done, I am no longer attached to who gave it to me. Conversely, I love the energy of a barter or exchange. It is significantly different. It has a vibration and lasting energy. The interaction and connection to the gifter has a ripple effect. For example, I bartered a mural with my friend Audra. Her roles in my life are wide and varied. Audra painted a mural of a vibrant poppy on our farm shed. We bartered one month's tuition in exchange for the poppy mural. This was done two years ago, but when I see it, I still feel joy because it's beautiful and reminds me of my talented and brilliant friend. The ripple effect of this barter continues to impact me every single day. What a payoff compared to the single tuition payment. I never have those feelings when looking at the numbers in my Venmo account.

We barter for other reasons as well. At Chavitos, we firmly desire access to alternative education so bartering can be a win-win way of making it accessible to more families. For me, it's a social justice-motivated decision to equal the playing field and to get more students of diversity into our programs. I also like the creativity that is involved in bartering. On our applications, we ask families what they would like to barter. Even if we don't barter with them right away, it is an informative snapshot into the deeper recesses of a person. What they include in that response tells me what giftings they not only could bring to the program, but to the world. When we know people beyond their occupations and primary roles, and we show an interest in their passions and talents, we are deepening the mycelium of our community.

For us, bartering is two-fold. Sometimes, we share a need we have. In the past, this included accounting support, sewing pillow cases, engineering how to move an RV, sharing cooked meals to lighten our weekly workload, bodywork to support a six-hour day in the forest, and yard work while we are out of the country for six months. Just like our needs change, barters can be short term or long. Other times, we ask families what skills they can share with us. We've bartered car oil changes, driving lessons, weekly loaves of warm sourdough bread, guitar lessons, personal training, house cleaning, rental management, family song circles, newsletter editing, family photo sessions, website support, and book publishing! When we get new families enrolled, I love dreaming about what ways we can barter for mutual benefit.

Parent Support & Education

Another driving value of the Chavitos Way is parent education. To best support our students, we need to use our professional experience and education to support their families. All parents need support, mentors, and advice. We express this value through our monthly email newsletter, parent/guide conferences, weekly learning points summarizing K-8 education, yearly book studies, and parenting classes. Let's dive deeper into the monthly newsletter and weekly learning points as tools for parent education and support.

Our newsletters include personal seasonal stories from our family, a book club pick that highlights work from child specialists like Dan Siegl, Dr. Becky, Joanna Faber, and Julie King, and behavioral support suggestions from important and often marginalized perspectives, like those of BIPOC and LGBTQA+ authors. I include Spanish resources like seasonal Spanish songs, games, or learning resources. My favorite part of the newsletter is highlighting community resources like local businesses or the work Chavitos parents are doing in their wider communities.

My intention in writing the newsletter is to help parents meet the needs of their children in nature and at home. It's a bridge between what students learn at Chavitos to applying the philosophy at home. It's a way for me to share the Chavitos philosophy in monthly, digestible snippets. The newsletter gives parents resources that hopefully lead to support the development of their children. We live in an era rife with neuroscience and research. Hopefully, the newsletter will give parents tools for their child-rearing toolkits.

I love hearing from families about how these newsletters impact them. I get numerous testimonies, from those as simple as families telling me they started to collect sunflower seeds from their garden so they can replant them next year, to more significant testimonials about parents learning their child is highly sensitive after using a digital assessment I shared with them. Or testimonials about family members being able to name parts of their experience as individuals when they previously couldn't. My hope is that our community is supported, educated, and improved through these monthly newsletters. Do you see parent education being a service you want to provide in your program?

Belonging

Another core value of The Chavitos Way is using rituals to teach students that everyone belongs. We focus on cultivating opportunities for children to explore and develop their identity, and to share their culture with those around them. Alongside our belief that a wealth of diversity should be present and celebrated, we also want children to see guides, other families, and other kids who look like them and identify as they do.

One of our preschool students, for example, has a mantra they repeat for empowerment. They say, "I'm proud to be Native." After a few months at the preschool, she independently added, "…like Jose." Jose is Mayan. He was born in Joyabaj, Quiche, Guatemala. I was thrilled this child could see and identify with another person about her indigeneity at such a young age. She has found belonging in an identity that all too often is stereotyped and disenfranchised in mainstream U.S. culture. Thankfully, Chavitos can be a setting where she can learn to take pride in who she is and find belonging.

At Chavitos, we have many practices we use to consciously celebrate diversity and build empathy among students. Some of the most prominent ways include:

- **Exploring family histories.** Kids are invited to research their family ancestors and share their family culture through our ritual of using Culture Bags. In this practice, students present to the class examples from their family culture, past and present. My kids, for example, have shared Chinese red envelopes, huipils from Guatemala, and the lore of selkie seals from their Scottish/Irish ancestors in their culture bags. Other students share current family traditions by bringing in a racing helmet, talking about family breakfast rituals, or sharing poetry. Regardless of what is shared, I have witnessed new friendships bloom after a cultural bag sharing as students realize they have more in common with their peers than they first realized.

- **Engaging in social justice learning.** We've learned how to honor the Puyallup Tribe, whose stolen land we are on. We arrange for Indigenous teachers to teach us about two-spirit, bead work, ribbon dancing, and salmon songs. We've also taught students about the history of redlining by reading primary resources of historical accounts, coloring in a map of Tacoma based on redlining practices, and locating where we each lived and which color zone we live in. We've also started learning about heroes and heroines of the modern age who are fighting climate change and systemic racism, as well as those who are reclaiming and practicing food sovereignty. We invite voices who are different from ours to teach us about how they are making a difference.

- **Expecting and modeling grace and courtesy.** We do this through modeling and expecting inclusion, sharing space with others, and teaching about how to take care of our bodies in all types of weather. We also teach children to respect other students' needs if they are different from our own. We don't shame or alienate those different from us and we openly talk about our neuro diversities as superpowers.

- **Allowing kids to lead.** When possible, we ask kids to take the lead in the teaching process. This might look like a few volunteers to support a group tour or lead a new student into their favorite part of the forest. Or, to show a new student where to hang their backpack or eat a snack. We ask kids to lead the morning circle and read to others who need support. Kids have the power to teach and lead their peers and guides.

- **Celebrating differences.** We believe that if everyone were the same, it would create a monoculture of life. To honor our differences, we use biographies and history to teach about cultural, neuro, and familial diversity. It's our firm belief that diversity is a superpower.

Embracing Neurodiversity

The last core value I want to share in this chapter is that of reframing
neurodiversity. Currently, one of the biggest types of diversity our program
supports is neurodiversity. The brain is easier to study now than it was in
the past, giving us life-changing information. Alternative care and education
programs, ours included, attract and are a safe haven for some families and
students with neurodiversity. At Chavitos, we celebrate our differences,
meaning we reframe neurodiversity as a superpower. We approach behaviors
with curiosity and have open conversations about how to best meet the
needs of individual students. Here are some practical ways we consciously
embrace neurodiversity and instigate healthy, open conversations with
neurodivergent families and students at Chavitos:

- **We include a thorough parent questionnaire in our enrollment
  packet.** Parents are the experts on their children, and we ask them
  for their wisdom from the very beginning. This honoring of their
  knowledge sets the tone for an effective partnership and gives
  guides a step up for knowing how to support the new student.
  We've started using questionnaires with specific questions about a
  child's temperament and personality with the intention of learning
  more deeply about that child. If parents can answer these types of
  questions with ease and clarity, then I find that those parents work
  well within the partnerships we set up with them and their children.
  By asking direct questions about any neurodiversity, the guide and
  parents work together before enrollment to create a successful plan
  for the child before they attend Chavitos. This might look like
  having the child wear a weighted vest during lessons or creating
  a special hand signal for when the child needs to take space in
  a calming area.

- **We hold space for self-advocacy.** Many adults in our current age are learning about their own neurodiversities. They are getting long overdue diagnosis and learning how to share their findings with their community. Many have started this process because of the new resources and language around neurodiversity. With this new language we can self-advocate and let others know what we and our children need. This self-advocacy can look like a conversation at pick up where information is passed along to a guide. For instance, I learned that carpooling was difficult for a family due to a parent's own sensitivity to oral stimulation during car rides. Self-advocacy could also look like a parent requesting email communication instead of a phone call since their brain doesn't process verbal information as well as other communication methods. I've noticed the parents who advocate for themselves also advocate for their child's needs around touch, personal boundaries, and learning styles. To help parents feel comfortable in sharing these details, we model self-advocacy and also share gratitude and acknowledge when it's being done by both parents and children. In all cases, we try to receive this information without attaching stigma to it and we continue the conversation about finding solutions that would work. Open dialogue has led our guides to find amazing out-of-the-box and non-conservative solutions to situations that have arisen.

- **We model language that supports self-advocacy.** To help create a community of self-advocates we need to learn the language around our capacities and conditions. Guides have training and continual conversation around neurodiversity so we can be educated about the current research. We learn about symptoms of being dysregulated and how this might show up in the classroom. Then, we share these

observations and learnings with the students through modeling and
direct lessons. We use and teach specific language in the classroom
by talking and reflecting together. By modeling to our children how
to advocate for themselves, we are teaching them that not only is it
okay to ask for help, but that we can love and accept those parts of
ourselves that are different from others and require accommodation.
We make it "cool" to take a work break or to bring a chewy necklace
to school by emphasizing it's awesome to know our bodies and what
they need for us to be successful learners. We also ask questions to
help guide students toward new language. When we see a child's
feet wiggling or if they look lethargic, we can stop and ask them
how their bodies feel and what they might need. Then, we can
let them meet their needs. Sometimes, we offer dialogue around
our observations.

> *"I'm seeing you slumped over your work and your arms are droopy.
> It looks like you're having a hard time holding the pencil and
> getting your poem written."*

> *"Do you think your body might need support in waking up a
> little? Do you know what activity you would like to do? Maybe
> swinging in the hammock or doing a run on the ninja line? Let
> me know what you think will help support your body."*

This is an example of not only helping children learn what
their body is trying to tell them, but it also models descriptive
language. We try to model the language we want our children
to use so they can adopt the same language — as a toolkit for

advocacy— for themselves whenever they're ready to do so. Here are some examples:

> *"I feel… and I need support with…"*
> *"I am… and it would really help me if…"*
> *"I need (space, a hug, comfort, to move my body etc.)"*

We use teaching tools to illustrate the more nuanced and advanced emotions of disgust, irritation, overwhelm, overjoy and nurturing. Our goal in modeling the use of language that allows us to self-advocate is to create a community where all members are held with gentleness and acceptance and where needs get met.

- **We hire neurodivergent** guides. The best guide is one who can understand and empathize with a child. Humans can be complex, and if a guide sees the world from a similar perspective or moves through the world with similar patterns (including psychological, emotional, and physical patterns) to those of the children in their care, they can respond to children with understanding and connection. They can also respond to situations with creative problem-solving techniques they might have already used successfully in their own lives. A guide who understands a child's diversity can create an environment where that child's needs will be met. Even better, guides can create an environment that predicts and prepares for those needs. Guides can create an environment where a child thrives, not just survives. For example, a guide can know the importance of a student swinging on a swing and let them naturally finish that movement instead of interrupting it to start a class on time. Or, during movement time, I child can opt for heavy work over play. In a classroom, we sometimes have weighted pillows, earmuffs, or fidget toys for students who need sensory stimulation to concentrate. The offering does not need to be extraordinary. We find that simply expanding our ideas of what "essential materials" are, or what choices are offered to a child, is enough.

- **We make accommodations.** We find that not only must we hold space for self-advocacy, model the use of language that supports self-advocacy, and hire guides who are attuned to children asking for what they need, *but we must also make accommodations based on children's requests.* To fail at following through on accommodating a child's request demonstrates that their voice is not important, that they don't know what their body needs, and that speaking up for themselves will not help them as they move through life. This happens all too often in our society. So, we make an effort at Chavitos to adjust our expectations, as educators, based on the specific needs of the children in our care. Sometimes, when an accommodation is requested, guides need to confirm with the program director or other adults in a child's care network that the accommodation being requested aligns with our long-term goal of molding empathetic, capable, brilliant adults who are out-of-the-box problem solvers and heartfelt advocates. It would be easy to let an eight-year-old have big emotions about a class he doesn't like, and refuse to go to class by hitting, screaming or tantruming. However, if we accommodated those behaviors, it might not be in that child's long-term interest. Here are examples of accommodations we often can and do make for children:

  ◦ We have community spaces like a classroom, mud kitchen and building space that can hold loud, high energy. Equally important is to create private spaces like a pillow loft, sand pit or single swing for children to retreat to when needing quiet, calm and low stimulation. If a child is feeling tired, they can create a nest of pillows and lay down during literacy. You would be surprised by how much concentration and reading a child can have when they listen to their bodies and take the space they need. Not all children will be doing the lesson in the same way.

- Honor children's timelines and flow state. If necessary, a student is welcome to stay where they are for as long as they need to be. Meaning, this could be the whole three hours of class if that's what they need. Trust that their body is recalibrating, processing, or adjusting to something and that is important work.

- If a child is hungry and it's not snack time, they can still get their food out and eat it. We don't have to wait until the designated time. We can eat when hungry. Students can even bring their snacks to their work area and munch while they learn. Children get hungry many times throughout the day, and we need to honor their requests for food. We don't say, "But you just ate." or "You can't be hungry yet, it's only 9:30." We teach them to listen to their bodies and to nourish them how they see fit.

- We give children choices about their gear. They can listen to their bodies and put on or take off gear however and whenever they need. Their bodies run differently than an adult body. They might be toasty warm when we are freezing. Let them control their temperature and learn how to add layers as they need. If we see a child is cold but they don't sense it, we can give them options. That might sound like, "Your nose is red, and your hands are stiff. Please put on some layers. You decide what layers."

○   We have routine and consistency with our schedule. If something
    new is added to our schedule, we will take time to prepare for
    it and talk about that change. We take time to answer questions
    and hold space for any processing.

Knowing our values can bring clarity to the programs we create, making
each program unique and ultimately, attracting others with the same values.
This makes it easier for us to live a counter-culture life. When others are
like-minded and walking with us, we can stay true on our path.

Invitations for Reflection

- What were your passions and interests as a child? Do you still enjoy those activities, hobbies, or people? What can this tell you about your values now, as an adult?

- When do you feel the most enraged? Can you strip away the circumstances of that situation and find the bones of what is left over? Does anything that remains point toward a value you hold?

- List your top three values. If you don't know what they are yet, consider the values expressed throughout this chapter and select a few that resonate with you. If those values aren't already woven into your everyday life or business, write two or three steps you can take to make them more central in your life.

- If there are people in your life who align with your values, how might you spend more time with them and create something with them?

Part 2

Foundational Practices

Chapter 5

Honor the child

Children love to hear stories, especially stories about their parents when they were their age. One story I tell my own children is about how I used to end playdates when I felt they were going too long. What I didn't know at the time, when I was ten years old, was that I was doing so because I am a Highly Sensitive person. In my youth, I didn't have the language to express my needs around being highly sensitive, other than to end an interaction. I was in the fourth grade, and my best friend Melissa lived in the neighborhood in a cul de sac one street over. One afternoon Melissa was over to play. We were in the upstairs toy room playing house. I was having fun, but suddenly something switched in me, and I wasn't enjoying our time together any longer. Everything she did was annoying and grated on me. The playdate was stretching too long and my emotional energy was drained. While I could sense these feelings in my body, I didn't know how to communicate that to Melissa. Setting a healthy boundary or a limit wasn't something in my skill set. From experience, I knew of one sure way to get her to leave: pick a fight and make her so mad she would leave. Then,

I could have the space and silence I needed. So, I initiated a fight and just like I'd planned, she got mad and left, storming home. I felt such relief at the quietness and spaciousness that resulted from the fight, but what an upsetting experience for Melissa.

CASE STUDY

This story was fresh on my mind as Keats and I planned his 10th birthday party. He drew the invitation for his friends and even wrote the details inside. As we planned, I could predict Keats would get overwhelmed with a 25-hour sleep over with six friends. I asked questions to help him become aware of this and was grateful he had expanded awareness around this due to past experiences and debriefings with me. As predicted, Keats also anticipated this potential burnout, so we had a long conversation and planned high energy activities, low energy activities, and brainstormed plans for how he could take space. Due to my own experience in social burnout, we set the tone of the birthday party by letting the kids know they could listen to their bodies and opt out of activities if they wanted. Whole group participation wasn't required. They could all take care of their needs as they wanted.

The children listened to this, and at one time during the party, I found two asleep on the couch, tucked under a blanket while others flowed in and out of gameplay with the boardgame on the kitchen table. A few other kids in the bedroom played another game. And as predicted, by the time pizza was on dinner plates, Keats was feeling done. His body was getting feverish and even achy. He headed to my bed, got snuggly, and took the rest of the night to himself. The party continued seamlessly with the kids continually adding to a pile of blankets and pillows in the living room for a movie and eventually, sleep.

As Keats and I snuggled and debriefed the next morning, I got to share with him about my own story of not knowing what to do when I had overextended myself with Melissa as a child. Keats and I celebrated how he took care of his body and talked openly about what he would have changed, kept, or added (highly sensitive people like to self-analyze and debrief about events in detail). Keats told me, "I don't think I can go to school tomorrow." I then shared one of my most useful tools with him: creating space. I told him I had intentionally scheduled space and rest for our whole Sunday. All we had to do that day would be nap, read, and play at home. I felt a release in Keats when he heard our day's plans. Then, we took a nap together. Sure enough, by Monday, he was recharged and ready for school, already making plans for next year's birthday party with less friends and a shorter timeframe.

You may be wondering, why veto the 25-hour birthday marathon? I could have easily prevented his overwhelm. But that would have been protecting him from discomfort that ultimately led to greater self-awareness and gaining a beneficial strategy that would come in handy throughout his life. I wanted him to feel what over-extension felt like. I wanted to guide him in future planning and teach him how to listen, use growing wisdom, and make plans that would support his specific needs. I wanted to model being intentional about recovery and how to plan and create space for rest, recuperation, and balance.

What would have been more powerful? Preventing the experience, or using the experience as a touchstone for future reference? Honoring our children and letting them discover themselves in their own ways is so important, even if it makes adults feel uncomfortable. We are in this for the long run and for bigger purposes. My favorite way to honor a child is to listen to them. When they say they are hungry, cold, scared or anything else, we should acknowledge what they're telling us. We need to show them we hear them.

"Okay. You are hungry."

"Yes, I can see you are cold, you're shivering."

"I can see that scares you. You look worried."

So often, we dismiss children. We don't even know we are doing it. We brush off their emotions with comments like,

"But you just ate."

"But the sun is out. I'm hot."

"Don't be scared. It's just a cartoon."

We need to stop doing this. Honor your child by accepting what they are telling you. Let's look more closely at seven detailed ways to honor the precious child in your life.

Set Age-Appropriate Expectations

It's important to know age-appropriate expectations. We don't want to expect too much of a child or too little. The tricky thing about this, though, is that we also need to grow and learn with the children in our lives while we manage our expectations for them. We can't expect a three-year-old child to do what a ten-year-old does. Setting that expectation would discourage a young child and make them feel like their contributions weren't valuable. Similarly, we can't expect a twelve-year-old to participate as a four-year-old would. This would stunt their growth and hold them back. Knowing your child and their temperament will help you find the sweet spot, but it also takes some learning, trial and error, and sometimes even crossing a boundary to then know where our limits lay (as opposed to where we thought they were).

Our programs see many opportunities during the school day to honor our children. Let's look at how to honor your child with clothing and getting dressed. The truth is, most of you are probably doing too much for your children in this arena. Generally, American families expect too much *emotional* maturity (not wanting tantrums or expecting sharing) from their kids and not enough *physical* maturity (helping with chores around the home). Spending time outdoors, for example, requires knowledge of layering clothing. This can mean more time and energy spent on getting dressed for nature school. Finding the right balance of clothing layers can be a lot to juggle for parents and kids. Often, it leads to declarations of, "I'm not going to school!" or "I don't like those pants, they are itchy." Here are some helpful tips for how to prevent meltdowns and how to encourage independence with this routine, while also getting them dressed for the weather appropriately:

- Elementary students can get themselves fully dressed and even remember to pack an extra pair of clothing, socks and base layers on their own. That capability is nourished by teaching younger children, preschool-aged children, how to get dressed. When we teach children to be more independent when they're younger, they demonstrate that independence when they're older.

- Preschool-aged students will need support at varying levels. They will need help at first, then they will let you know when they are ready to do it themselves. They are so great at communicating this. They might say, "I want to do it!"

- Keep a child's forest clothes separate from their other clothing. Make it accessible, like in a basket under their bed or in a separate drawer.

- Set aside extra time in the morning, or the night before, for children to complete "getting ready tasks" on their own, without the stress of a time constraint. They will feel so proud of their accomplishments, and you will enjoy the free time to take care of your own personal needs. It might take them twenty minutes to get their wool sock over their heal, but that's okay.

- Ignore backwards pants and shirts or inside-out garments. We aren't aiming for perfection. We are aiming to build confidence and let children have a choice in how they wear their clothing. Expectations of perfection can make a preschooler feel discouraged and resent their forest clothes. It might result in a lot of whining, tantrums, and refusals.

- If a child doesn't want to put on the pants, give them a choice, "You do need to wear pants today, but you can decide which color! Do you want pink or blue pants?" Or "These are your pants for the day, do you want to wear them inside out or tag in?"

- Make it playful. Use voices or characters to help make it fun. My child used to love it when a sweet fairy voice gave them choices about which socks to choose. Other days, the clothing itself would be wild and animated and need the child to help wrangle it or teach it how to behave.

Lessons about independence in clothing and knowing what to expect for each age group can easily be extended to how children contribute around the home and at school. Our family has a tradition around birthdays. We celebrate our kids getting older by introducing a new privilege (going around the block by themselves, staying up 15 minutes later, starting to play a virtual math game) and we expect a new responsibility (washing their own clothes, putting away the silverware, hanging up their backpack and emptying their snack trash).

One year, when our youngest child was turning six, she was really struggling with the number of chores she had. This would end in tears, with worrisome comments like, "I'm running late. I'm not going to finish." Doing chores turned each peaceful morning into an emotional ticking time bomb. I observed this over time and realized two things. First, if she couldn't do a task and was asking for help, I could support her by modeling and re-teaching her how to do the task. This doesn't mean I did the whole task for her. It meant I could use my proximity to be closer, answer questions, and give sweet reminders like, "That's a spoon. Spoons go with spoons." In our adult mind, putting silverware away is an easy job, it's just sorting three different objects. But, for a six-year-old, it can be a challenge. I found myself asking, "What does she need to be successful with the chore?" What we came up with was providing a stool and teaching her how to bring it over to the counter. We would move the silverware from the dishwasher to the counter for her. We stopped reminding her and instead let her tend to it when she was ready. Our agreement was that the chore had to be completed before bedtime. Also, for my child, I helped her put the silverware away until she told me, "I got it, Mama." I focused on teaching her the steps to accomplish the task and then honoring her systems. She liked to move all the forks together, then spoons. Gradually, I reduced my support and eventually, just stood near her while she did it. I supported her with handling the sharp knives, or only when she asked for help. Soon, she could do it all on her own and was speedy, as well.

In addition to setting appropriate expectations, we also must adjust our expectations. When my youngest child turned seven, we decided not to add a new responsibility to her daily routine. I could see the ones she already had were enough, and we wanted her to feel successful with her contribution to our family. We didn't want her to feel overwhelmed. Just as we did, give yourself permission to change the chores and shift your expectations. Sometimes, our kids will ask to trade a chore for one they are bored with or ones they don't enjoy doing. When this happens, remember: the goal is to honor the child by seeing them as an important contributing member of the family. Daily and weekly chores are a way to include them in the organization and flow of a shared space. Some home chores could be:

- Dusting shelves
- Wiping down windows
- Putting toys in baskets
- Matching socks
- Setting the table
- Helping unpack the groceries
- Cutting vegetables
- Unloading the dishwasher
- Folding towels
- Making the bed
- Putting folded clothes in drawers
- Organizing stuffies

We have these same expectations in the forest and farm. Many parents have testified to how they saw an increase in their children's independence and involvement in their home due to the expectations we set in the forest. Students get used to being in charge of their backpacks, lunchboxes, and gear. Then, that responsibility naturally transfers to home and to their toys, shoes, and jackets. Some forest and farm chores could be:

- Returning tools to their space
- Putting away mud kitchen supplies
- Finding ropes and rehanging them
- Moving wood chips to bare spots
- Sweeping sheds and gazebos
- Weeding patches
- Mulching garden beds
- Cleaning the composting toilet
- Brushing goats
- Filling animal water
- Returning wagons
- Picking up trash and lost clothing items

If we want your children to meet our expectations, we need our requests around the home and school to be appropriate for what they can physically and mentally do. As adults, we can invite children into experiences with us. While we observe their participation, we can adjust our expectations to make the task at hand easier or more challenging, all the while knowing that each child will have a varying degree of involvement. A three-year-old might complete a task in a short spurt of time before getting distracted or feeling the task is complete. An older elementary-aged child can sustain focus and see a task through to completion. When we know what is appropriate to expect, we can offer intriguing tasks and request a child's expectations for involvement.

Teach Self-Care

At Chavitos we expect children to take care of their bodies with love and respect, and to treat others' bodies with kindness and gentleness. In addition, we model and guide them to love the space they are in, to feel ownership of it, and to tend to its greatest good. It's important to take care of our own bodies, our space around us, and those who share it with us. We aim to raise adults who are aware of their impact and who want to be conscious of how they interact with and leave spaces. When taught this at a young age, children grow up to be adults who can apply the same self-care principles to all sorts of objects in their lives, including businesses and committed partnerships.

There is intention layered into many of the details of our learning environment at Chavitos, from what clothing brands we request parents to use, what materials we bring into the classroom, and how our spaces are set up. In our programs, we use natural materials that are beautiful and inspire us to care about their upkeep. For example, at our farm, we use recycled glass jars that hold fresh flowers on each table. One of the farm chores is to replace the flowers and water and make sure they look fresh. The first year of our program, the jars would get broken frequently. So, we had lessons on how to place the flower jars in the center of a table and how to be mindful of where our bodies were moving. We also taught the kids how to safely sweep and dispose of glass shards. We provided kid-sized brooms and dustpans. The first few practices of this were hard and felt cumbersome. They felt like an interruption to our rhythm. I would cringe each time I heard the shattering of glass nearby. It would have been easier for guides to step in and fix or clean it themselves. It seemed like every other minute I would hear the crash of another glass jar. But, months into our program, we didn't have any more broken jars, and I heard kids remind each other to be mindful of the glass jars, to move them away from the table's edges. This is a lesson that could have been deemed too time-consuming or unimportant, but I saw it as an essential lesson about how to care for and tend to all our things. By using glass, a breakable material, we teach the kids to care and be mindful of what makes up their environment. We want to raise humans who are aware of the components around them, both living and nonliving. We want them to be mindful about how they interact and engage with things around them, and to know they have an impact on those things.

Here are some tips on how to honor your child while teaching self-care:

1. Have kid-sized supplies at hand. Brushing with a long, heavy broom will lead to frustration and quick declarations that sweeping is dumb. It will also lead to bonked heads and poked eyes with an unwieldy broom handle. But having a smaller, lighter broom will be more manageable, special and inviting.

2. Prepare age-appropriate activities in which kids can see immediate results of their actions, such as dusting, mopping, sharpening pencils, or picking up books.

3. Focus on the process, not the end-product. Kids get distracted and their focus can bounce around. So, expect them to do the work for shorter spurts of time. When they say they are done, don't try to convince them to do more. Acknowledge their work. "Great. I see you put away the shovels. They will be ready to dig with tomorrow. Thank you."

4. Use open-ended requests to the whole group, such as, "I see some pillows left out, who can stack those straight?" Someone

will always volunteer. If no one does, just wait until someone volunteers. It might seem like an eternity before they do, but, if I just wait a little longer, making everyone a little more uncomfortable with the weight of the unmet request, someone will jump in and get the job done.

5. Be grateful for their contribution no matter what it looks like. Showing gratitude for kids' work and sharing the big picture of the impact of their contribution will help them see they are helping their community. Try statements like, "Wow! I appreciate your hard work. Now our space is ready for the next class!"

6. Offer choices. With younger kids, give them two choices. "Green mittens or blue? T-shirt inside out or right side out?" With older kids, offer more options and wider boundaries.

7. Have agreements that put responsibility on the children. One way we do this is by not lifting children up or down from a tree. If they want to climb the tree, they need to get up and down by themselves. We're around to guide children with advice, but they need to learn to be in their body, trust their body, and know nature.

8. Make it fun. Kids love to learn through play. Make them robots who are mechanically moving around. Use silly voices. Or make an object speak. "I'm left out and so lonely. All the other shovels are resting at home. Please put me away." Make your request a game. "How many pieces of paper can we find?" or "I spy an object on the ground that's white, who can find it?"

Respect Their Pace

Let children live at their own pace. Most preschool-aged children do things slowly. At that age, they are still building up their muscle memory and ability to do tasks that older children and adults do much quicker. For example, zipping a jacket could probably be done quicker by a sloth than by most preschoolers learning the pinch grip and the ability to thread the small plastic into the zipper hole. But don't rush them, or any children. And, if we take over and do the task for them, we rob them of the complete joy and satisfaction of self-accomplishment. How many of us have heard the declaration, "I did it!" This statement is usually the result of a magical moment of celebration. When we let children do activities at their own pace, we give them the gift of experiencing completion and reward for hard work. This means we need to change our pace to match theirs. If we are on a walk and they stoop down to look at a bug, you do the same. Match their pause. Don't keep walking. They are giving you an invitation to enter into a state of wonder. Sometimes, kids move faster than us, shouting, "Let's run! Chase me!" Try to match this energy. Accept their invitation to get blood pumping and muscles moving. See if you can find a way to engage with them at their pace in a way that honors your body, as well.

Sometimes, a child's pace doesn't match that of the group. That is okay. You can still honor their pace by checking-in with them. "How do you feel about this activity? Is there something else you would rather do? Is there anything else your body needs?" This encourages children to listen to their body, to honor their pace, and to not compare themselves to what is happening around them. In every game or activity there are ways to honor where a child is at. They can take a wiggle break and run to the forest, do five jumps, or twist in the hammock. They can take a slow stroll around the cedar trees or dip their feet into the pond. They can take their work to a quiet, shady spot and work alone. Or they can invite a friend to talk about their work in a space far from the big group, working quietly. By asking the child what they need, you're letting them come up with solutions. This shows them they know best how to honor their body. Honoring a child's pace is also a simple way we can live consciously. When we prepare our minds to be open and observant of the children we serve, we can work together to meet any needs.

Let Them Flow

Letting children "flow" is similar to honoring a child's pace, but it's a little different. It is more about honoring a state of meditation and deep focus. Flow was made popular by Hungarian American Psychologist, Mihaly Csikszentmihaly (1990). It is a state of mind where we get lost in the activity at hand. All else fades away and we are absorbed in the task in front of us. I love entering flow, as it feels easy and light. But it feels horrible to be called out of it abruptly, like when a warm blanket is snatched off you. That can be alarming. So, whenever possible, we should create an environment that honors a child's need to be in their flow. Let them focus and enter into deep play, the kind where the whole world fades away. Don't interrupt them. If they want to play with a pinecone for an hour, let them. We used to have a student who would sit in the rain at the greenhouse edge and watch a raindrop fall and hit the wood's edge. Who knows what engineering principles were being discovered or pondered in those moments. We silently moved around him, not breaking his concentration and letting him join the group when he was satisfied and ready to move on.

If a child is really interested in something, a guide should increase their distance, allowing the child to make the choice to focus more intently on something independently. Only when invited should adults interrupt, offer observations, or engage or play with a child. Otherwise, let them flow uninterrupted. Trust that they are learning from observing. By letting them choose their own activities, we teach students to learn to listen to their bodies at a young age. It's a radical act, to teach kids at a young age to trust themselves and to do the activities or movements they need to at any given moment. Adults don't need to know why a child is doing something, they just need to trust that children can do it.

Parents can learn to reflect that back to children. After a child is done playing, we can say, "I saw your face beaming with joy as you held that baby bunny. How did that feel?" or "Your face was all scrunched up in concentration during that math activity. What were you thinking or feeling?" By not interrupting the flow state, we are preventing meltdowns and bursts of anger. We are instead having forethoughts and creating a space of peace, focus and learning. We are creating an opportunity for a child to experience focus, lack of self-consciousness, enjoyment, and persistence. In the long run, we are creating humans who can cope with life's stressors, have fewer distractions, less self-judgment, greater motivation to finish a task, and the ability to spend longer on a task.

Invitations for Reflection

- Consider whether you match your child's pace at some point during your day together. If you don't, what activities might offer opportunities for you to do so?

- When do you enter flow? How do you feel when you are in it?

- Think about a time when you interrupted a child's flow. What was their response?

- What strategies do you use to gently guide children out of flow?

- What are some responsibilities you want a child's support with?

- Consider the responsibilities children in your life have. Do they struggle with those responsibilities? Why? How can you support them in those instances?

Chapter 6
Establish Healthy Learning Environments

Change Your Language

As adults we have the opportunity to be wordsmiths. A small tweak in our language can bring honor to a child. Or a small shift in the other direction can bring shame and blame, leading a student to shut down or to damaging our connection. As guides, we can rephrase the direction we give so that it makes a child feel in control, seen, and ready for action. Some of the phrases guides can use to honor a child include:

Instead of, "You are cold, put on a jacket please."
Try, "Does your body need anything to feel good right now?"

Instead of, "You are so wiggly and you're distracting me."
Try, "I see a wiggly body. What do you need right now?"

Instead of, "Don't yell at me."

Try, "Your voice is loud and strong. Do you want to share how you are feeling?"

Instead of, "You can't hit."

Try, "You are upset. Hitting hurts. Do you want space or support?"

Instead of, "Stop talking during my lesson."

Try, "I can do my best teaching with a silent class."

By using questions, sharing observations, and sharing our feelings, we are modeling introspection for children and stoking their empathy. Hopefully, they will start to ask themselves the same questions we've been asking and will become aware of how their choices are making others feel. By shifting our questions, we are also replacing blame and judgment, which can limit a child from expressing how they feel and lead to wrong assumptions or information being taken in. We want to replace blame with curiosity, an open heart to learn, and an environment of acceptance and safety. This open space leads to deeper learning of who others are and can shed light on a situation we can all learn from. This leads to deeper discoveries and doesn't have a fixed outcome. Children who are spoken to in this way will become adults who speak to others this way, too.

Since a parent's and guide's outer voice becomes a kid's inner voice, we want to use the questions and reframe information in ways that model self-talk. By modeling self-talk and curiosity, we teach children to approach a situation with others or themselves with a human touch, with consideration for themselves and others. This work is preventive. It creates people who pay attention to their inner dialogue and who will speak to each other and their children with curiosity, kindness, and clarity.

Teach with Mantras

We want children to have a growth mindset. Mantras offer this. We start children young. Our goal is to reinforce mantras to the point that when children are adults, they still use mantras to get through difficult situations. We start teaching mantras with our youngest students, those who are around two years old, and continue this practice through elementary and middle school years. Mantras might come in handy when a three-year-old is climbing a tree, or when a ten-year-old is taking a standardized test.

We want mantras to be empowering and encourage reflection. Mantras allow our teachings to happen without adults or guides having to re-teach an entire lesson. The mantras are touchstones that you and your children can come back to when you're older. Don't be surprised if your children start repeating your mantras to you. If they do, open discussion about the topic at hand. Here is a short list of mantras we have adopted at Chavitos:

- Big sticks in big spaces.
- I can do hard things.
- I belong at Chavitos.
- Big emotions come and go.
- Big picture / Big perspective.
- Who has the power? Who doesn't have the power?

In a sense, mantras allow you to start building muscles to think and talk about big ideas and thoughts. Hold space for your children to talk about hard topics that come along with these mantras. Later, when you say the mantra again, doing so will trigger memories and thoughts within your child. This is how you create a library of information about that mantra, and memories of actions the child has already taken regarding the topic at hand. In this way, the mantra comes alive when your child repeats it. It then becomes muscle memory so they can repeat a skill or lesson without all the work of being retaught. Soon, they'll be doing the actions associated with the mantra without knowing it because they've internalized the mantra's meaning. This impacts and trickles down into their entire way of life.

Cultivate Collaboration

Another way our work can be preventive is by creating an organized system that is collaborative. Often, our systems are hierarchical with one "top dog" in the lead and others in rank and file, doing their bidding and work. There is little room for questions or multiple paths or ideas, and one voice is often the loudest and most demanding. But in Chavitos programs, we want to prevent one voice from ruling the rest. Our goal in honoring children is to create a system and organic structure of a round table where all are equals. All ideas have space to be shared and heard. All dreams are considered and entertained. All questions have a chance to be spoken. We sit in a circle (in which we all are seated at the same level), so we all have a voice and an opportunity to see everyone around us clearly. We make decisions that affect those we face in the circle. Guides and parents are on the same level as a child.

Outside of Chavitos, the structures of our current systems do not include children, elderly, BIPOC, or LGBTQIA+ individuals. Their voices and opinions aren't taken seriously. There is no space or opportunity to consider the rationale or brilliance of one considered too young, too old, or too different to contribute. But within our Chavitos programs, all ideas are equally important and can be held in this container. A child's idea is listened to, considered, and honored just as much as that of their guides. There is no one at the top. For meaningful and lasting change in our homes, we can also set up structures and rhythms to create space for all voices to be heard. By listening, we learn about their fears, anxieties, and joys, all of which are important to understanding them as individuals and getting a sense of how to advocate for and support them. I invite you to ask yourself the following questions regarding cultivating collaboration within any group or community you are a part of:

- Does the program we are a part of, or the group of learners within it, include pathways to talk about what is bothering us?

- Are there opportunities here for children to offer feedback to guides and to each other?

- Does everyone in the community, both guides and children, know how to offer feedback in ways that are constructive, informative, and lead to change? Or do our systems of communication only hold space for happy and joyful feelings? Are there also opportunities to share frustration, disappointment and anger?

- Do they have opportunities to *see* conflict, repair and mending? Do we give them opportunities to *process* with us? Do Guides and students have language to *engage* in conflict, repair, and mending? Do they see adults using this language?

- Do we have systems at home and in our programs that give everyone a chance to share until they feel complete? Or is the spotlight only given to those with the most power or those who are most outspoken and gregarious? Does quiet reflection have a place of

honor in our community? How do we hear the voice of those who
are more quiet, shy, and slower processors?

- When others are sharing do we show active listening with head
  nods, eye contact, and thoughtful questions or responses when
  they are done?

Sitting in a circle with no direct lead will encourage all voices to have
a say and impact. It's an excellent way to create a shared power situation.
One way our family and K-8 program likes to practice sitting in a circle
together and holding space for and honoring each other is through the
practice of "Rose, Bud, Thorn, (Aloha Foundation, 2020)" borrowed from
the Waldorf tradition. Rose, Bud, Thorn, is a method of checking-in with
people about the good, bad, and promising experiences they might have
faced during any given day. During the check-in, participants each share a
single rose, bud, and thorn with others. Here's a short description of what
these words signify within the scope of the check-in conversation:

- Rose: something that brought you joy, something you loved, or
  something you are celebrating about your day.

- Thorn: something that was challenging or difficult during your day.
  Or something that made you sad or frustrated.

- Bud: something you are looking forward to or want to accomplish
  in the future; something you plan on doing soon; something that
  offered "promise" during your day.

My family tries to practice Rose, Bud, Thorn around the kitchen
table during meals, especially dinner, since we've all been to different
places during the day. Honestly, sometimes by dinnertime, I've reached

my saturation point and I'm easily overstimulated with sound, including conversations. Around our table, you might find me wearing my noise canceling headphones (without music) to help regulate my nervous system. But I also know our time at the dinner table is a sacred time. I'm always interested to see my family's interpretation of the day. The simple ritual of sharing talking time allows me to become more available to my children during our meal. This simple ritual also invites deeper conversation about what we're experiencing out in the world.

Another reason I love this tradition is because it's very easy for us as parents to fall into dominating the conversation about our days when talking with our kids. But it's no fun for children to sit silently while an adult blabs on and on about the meetings, bills, or money that make up their days. The Rose, Bud, Thorn practice lets children know they will have a turn to talk. They can share and take up as much space as they need to debrief their experiences.

The Rose, Bud, Thorn tradition provides a structure to share a wider array of emotions and offers a path to balance our highs and lows. As you share with those in your own circle, notice: does your child have a balance of roses and thorns? Does your modeling bring connection to the family? Can you easily identify things you're looking forward to? Are your goal-related buds realistic and doable?

In the past, I noticed one of our kids only ever mentioned roses. He would often say, "I didn't have any thorns." This might have been because he loves school. It could also be that he doesn't want to focus on thorns. Maybe conflict was uncomfortable for him. Maybe he was worried about hurting my feelings (since I'm his guide and the director of his school) and doesn't want to share a thorn about a lesson I've recently taught. When he only shared roses, if I felt the moment was right and I had enough capacity to be a support for him, I'd push back and bring up a challenge I saw him move through that day. I asked,

"How did it feel when you and your friend got into a fight during soccer? I know you've been struggling with his high level of intensity during play."

Then, he might add, "Oh yeah, that was a thorn."

Even if he drops the conversation at that point, having brought up a thorn and having shown interest in his thoughts about it opens the door for him to potentially share, vent, and ask for support if he wants it.

For younger children, modeling this type of reflection is important. Our youngest has seen us doing this since she was a baby. When she was just learning to talk, she shared in gibberish with a fully animated face and wildly expressive arms telling a very important story that only she fully understood. The fact that we didn't exactly know what she was saying didn't matter to any of us. She loved having her very own turn to share and boy, did she have things to say. We would listen silently, Jose and I, smiling at each other across the table, sharing this moment of magic together. We were both surprised our child understood she had a turn just like her brother, mom and dad did. As she got a little older, her rose, bud, and thorn began to always be the same. "I love Mama. I love Papa. I love Mano (the nickname for the word hermano)," she would say. Then, she would listen to her brother share. Now, at seven-years-old, she shares details of her day and even though I'm with her for half of her day, I still learn new things every time. She still shares with passion and big expressions, and I love hearing her reflection about her day. I learn so much about what is important to her or what makes her worried. Regardless of age and what a child is sharing, we should try to model interest and deep listening.

To keep this practice reflective and sacred, it's important to notice our internal responses to what a child shares without immediately reacting to them. A simple, "Thank you for sharing, that seemed difficult for you." Or "Thank you for sharing, those are some good insights," are sufficient. Then move on. This is a time for connecting through listening, not problem solving. If you feel the urgent need to solve a problem, then ask for permission first. "I can see this upset you. Would you like some support in finding a solution?" I hope you can try this practice out, as it's a beautiful, simple way to honor your child at all stages of life . And if you practice it often, it may become a touchstone of connection for your family. Imagine a world in which everyone has an invitation to be in a circle of friends and share. Doing so can release pressure, inspire new ideas, and create deep, attuned listeners who hold attention for voices different than our own.

Make Space for All Emotions

The best way to prevent a tantrum and breakdown in a child is to acknowledge their feelings. This doesn't just mean happy, easy-to-accept feelings, but *all feelings*, including irrational, indecipherable feelings. It's important for children to know they are safe to have all emotions. A few months ago, I was at the pool with Jose. We watched a family swimming with their elementary-aged child in the pool. The parents were motivated to teach their child to put their head under water. The child was panicking, with wild tears, visible fear, and anxiety. They even repeated declarations of "No!" I kept hoping their parents would listen and stop, but they insisted and continued their mission for about an hour. I saw rigidity. The parents had a plan and goal and were lost to the reality that this wasn't working or benefiting the child. The joy of a summer swim and water exploration was quickly overshadowed. So often, as parents, we have an agenda like this.

We get consumed by the end goal and the process becomes traumatizing, miserable, and unproductive for children. In the case mentioned above, honoring the child could have looked like a shorter practice time, play interwoven into the working, asking the child if they had an idea of how to practice putting their head under the water, or creating a game of fun and safety in which the child is the boss for a moment before changing roles. The parents could also have been honest with the child about why this task was so important to them. What if they had used a story of mermaids or otters, inviting imagination and shapeshifting into the task? Maybe if the child was a baby otter swimming on their parents' belly, they would have been happier to put their head in the water.

At Chavitos, we believe in deeply listening to our students. One of the ways to do this is to make space for all emotions and use the emotions present to give us information. If I see boredom during a lesson, I take it as a clue to me to pick up the pace, insert a whole-body activity, and to check in with the students. The emotions on their faces and body language are inputs about lessons if we tune in and pay attention to what we observe. As guides, we follow their lead when setting the pace of lessons or the direction of a lesson. We observe their response to what we present. A lit-up face with clapping hands and bubbly joy is a sign that we are going in the right direction. We follow high energy and excitement and make compromises when that energy shifts.

Many of us adults didn't have anyone modeling how to manage complex emotions. We might have been told we were too loud, too much, or too extreme. And we might have been punished, isolated, or reprimanded for having complex emotions. But this leads to feelings of shame. On the contrary, being "too loud" can be helpful when we have an important message the world needs to hear. Being "too much" results in beautiful art and new ideas, pushing the boundaries and the boxes we live in. Being "too extreme" could mean we discover new realms of living and expand the possibilities within the frameworks of our lives.

Over the last few years, I've been thinking a lot about these emotions, especially anger. Anger is always trying to teach and tell us something. Anger is often mislabeled and misunderstood. But, when we reframe anger as "a messenger," we can grow into new realms, make changes to rebalance and bring calm, and define a moral that is important to us. David Whyte explores the concept of anger as a form of self-compassion in his book *Consolations: The Solace, Nourishment and Underlying Meaning of Everyday Words* (2015). In the essay titled "Anger," Whyte sees anger as a form of self-compassion that arises to protect and inform us of where we need new agreements in our life. Tending to those places is a form of self-compassion.

For me, when anger comes up, it means I need to examine my boundaries and perhaps set a clearer one. It can mean my values don't match my own or someone else's actions, and I need to make a change. It might mean I'm noticing something that isn't comfortable, and I might want to challenge the current status quo. Recently, anger has been telling me to reset my boundaries. One of our employees was called into jury duty with short notice. The jury duty lasted over four months. Each time my employee had to step away for jury duty, I found myself needing to hustle to find solutions. My anger around the situation was building towards a feeling of limited bandwidth and not wanting any other distractions from other pressing matters in my workday. My anger pointed out to me where I felt supported, and where I was lacking support. My anger informed me of my need for rest.

As a new generation of parents, we have choices around how we respond to "negative emotions" that arise in ourselves and our children. We can reject the notion of "bad emotions" and instead, we can view all emotions as tools. We can get curious about those emotions, name what we see, and ask questions about what is needed. We can foster a sense of self-awareness and acceptance to find out what message the emotions are telling us.

Embrace Diversity

If we look at nature, we see the ecosystems with the most diversity thrive. It's in environments of mono crops or where one element is dominant that we begin to see imbalance and disease. Conversely, nature teaches us the gift of diversity. I've seen how diversity in my life brings growth to our mindsets, perspective to our opinions, and health to our hearts. My first year teaching Montessori in a public school in Tacoma, I had a student named Yousef whose family had recently immigrated from Iraq. Yousef's best friend in class was Aiden. Aiden's father had fought in Iraq. Often, I would observe them learning together, huddled over a book, and think about these two children learning and playing together. These moments of play could unify and change their individual lives. They could build a friendship that nourished them both, despite differing beliefs and biases already rooting in these children's minds from shared stories they overheard from parents or on the news. There is power in becoming friends with someone from cultures and places in which past generations demonized each other and/or fought. This is the gift of diversity. When we put a face to the stereotypes we have built up, and they can't withstand, those old beliefs begin to dissolve. This is one of many reasons it's essential to create environments with as much diversity as possible. When we live our life with others, especially people of different races, sexual orientations, religions, backgrounds, or identities, we grow empathy. And empathy is an important tool children need to have in their toolkits and practice using from a young age.

Research shows that children notice differences and similarities in their caretakers at a very young age (Severson, 2020). This means they show a preference for faces that look like their main caregiver. Meaning babies can tell a difference in skin color and defining facial features. Cultivating diversity in our spaces, whether it be among our students, guides, or farmers at Chavitos, fosters acceptance and belonging. It also encourages curiosity and openness. Even in farming, we find that diversity of crops and flora is best for the land and the plants grown on it.

Diversity isn't all roses and ease. When living and learning with others different than us, we may come to various levels of discomfort. Our human brain is hardwired to not stick out, but to camouflage and be hidden in the pack, instead. We are herd animals that use blending-in to survive. So, sometimes, when we see diversity, it sends an alarm to our brain that the diversity we see endangers the whole pack. This discomfort is an ancient and extreme instinct that used to help people survive and not be picked-off by our predators. But we no longer need to carry that lesson, or those fears, forward in our societies.

CASE STUDY

When my oldest son, Keats, was five years old, he had a difficult time with another student at Chavitos. The other student's name was Drago. Drago was beautifully eccentric. They talked slowly, dragging out their words as long as possible. They were obsessed with rocks and had interesting observations about them. Their whole vibe irritated Keats, who was fast, impulsive, and a bold leader among the kids at school during play. Keats was experiencing someone

incredibly different than himself. It was easy for him to
"other" Drago. I was so grateful Drago gave Keats the
opportunity to bump against something, or someone, that
made him uncomfortable.

It would have been easy to separate these two boys,
moving Keats to a different group and encouraging them
both to play with other people. But I saw the discomfort as
an opportunity for the children's growth. I wanted to use
this situation as an opportunity for learning. I decided to
ask questions to the whole group of students during play.

"Drago, how do you feel when you are the tagger so
often when playing tag?"

"Keats, how do you think Drago feels when he isn't
given a turn to use the ladder?"

"Who has the most power in this situation?
Who doesn't have power? How can the person holding
power share it?"

Later, at home, Keats and I did emotional labor
together, untangling these big feelings inside him. I repeated
questions like those above and continued having at-home
discussions with Keats for many weeks. Sometimes, when
we left for school, we would talk about some of the things
we loved about Drago. Drago was creative and had fun
ideas. He was also adaptable and open to taking on roles
in play which he didn't really love. He was funny, too, and
often made us laugh with his surprising comments.

With this two-pronged guidance of giving Drago
space to share feelings, and leading Keats towards a
considerate friendship that holds space for serving,

instead of dominating, the boys' dynamic shifted. I was so
grateful that my child had this opportunity to experience
diversity and grow from someone different than himself.
Fast forward five years and I now see how that experience
was a touchstone, a lesson that impacted Keats deeply.
Keats now responds with heaps of empathy and curiosity
towards others who are different from himself. He knows
how to make exceptions to the rules for someone who is
neurodiverse. He knows how to be aware of those who are
being othered and will use his voice to bring awareness
and inclusion. I believe this empathy and curiosity
were nurtured in preschool at Chavitos. This is just one
example of how we can intentionally build community
around diversity.

Open-mindedness, especially as it relates to diversity, is a muscle.
Like all other moral intelligence characteristics, open-mindedness needs to
be modeled, practiced, and strengthened. Naturally, our somatic instinct
for survival is to surround ourselves with people who align with us and
who limit risk and discomfort. This is human nature. But giving in to this
instinct at all times can lead to discrimination and bias. And it can create a
superiority complex within us if we aren't careful. Instead of giving in to the
instinct, we should ask ourselves questions about the people and situation
at hand when we feel discomfort come up. Here are some examples
of self-inquiry:

- While there are many things I don't like about this person, what are
  the things I *do* like?
- What are this person's amazing and unique abilities and gifts?

- What can this person teach me?
- Is my view of this person limiting or restricting them in any way?
- If I'm the one with more power in this dynamic, am I using my power to suppress, harm, or dim this person's light?

- What do I have in common with this person and can I invite them to do that with me?
- What about myself frustrates this person? Am I open to changing or adapting to make them feel better or more supported?

These are the same questions I guide my students through in both our farm and forest spaces. If we model and teach children to ask these questions, they will be so much more fluid with discomfort and triggers than previous generations have been. Ultimately, this practice of self-inquiry around discomfort will lead to a more accepting and loving world, one where certain people or groups are not targeted, hated, or feared. If we're lucky, one of the children who practices empathy, curiosity, and self-inquiry will become a national leader or innovator of our medical, educational, or mental health systems. Or, they will be in a powerful position to model the same qualities to the rest of their communities, or even the world. Ultimately, the end goal of creating diverse settings for youth is world peace.

Acknowledge Injustice

Not only do we, as adults, have opportunities to talk to young children about diversity, but we also have the responsibility to teach them about the injustice that happens when we don't have spaces that honor diversity. Young children are already seeing and being impacted by racism, sexism, ableism, and "othering." As grown-ups in their lives, we should not avoid topics we think are confusing, scary, or sad. We should help them understand and navigate these topics and feelings instead of ignoring or dismissing them. As stewards of young minds, we must learn how to explain racism, sexism, ableism, and all other isms in our own words. This will help us find the right words to explain nuanced topics to young children and follow their lead when they have questions about them.

Call out all these isms as they manifest in your own life and continue to discuss them openly with your children. This will help children do the same as they grow. Young children are fully capable of understanding, naming, and addressing structural racism, but only if we support them in that process. What does it mean that racism is a system of power? How do we talk about white privilege in a way that a three-year-old might be able to understand? Why do most of the books available define racism interpersonally? These are just some of the questions we must answer for ourselves and be willing to address with our children, using words and concepts they can understand.

To undo injustice, we must actively participate in actions that work against it, in whatever form that injustice takes. There are so many ways to do so! We can brainstorm ideas with our children and start carrying out that work within our communities. Remember, young children learn more by watching what we do than by listening to what we say about our beliefs. Here are some ideas of ways to engage in work that promotes justice, anti-racism, and diversity with young children:

- Bring children to protests. Have them make their own sign. In most places, there are probably groups of people already working together to advance racial justice and advocate for anti-racist policy changes. Find these people in your city or workplace and get involved!

- Read books and diversify home libraries so all perspectives and narratives are present. Books and news resources help to keep the conversation going. Preview the book ahead of time to get a sense of the ideas and topics children might talk about.

- Ensure diverse representation is present in toy collections at home. Do you have dolls with different skin colors? Do you play out storylines with diverse family dynamics, like families with two moms or a single parent? Expand the storylines in books to represent different types of families. *Maybe the three bears had two dads. Maybe the dad cooks porridge. Maybe Goldilocks uses "they/ them" pronouns and returns the next day to make amends with the bears.* It is possible to change and diversify any story.

- Teach children about their ancestors. Have ancestor's pictures up and share stories of the food and cultures they belong to. Get curious and investigate family ancestry with children.

- Live your ancestral culture. Find songs, food, or rituals that your family's ancestors practiced and enjoyed. Try them out. In my life, for example, I've learned to listen to my body's cravings for rice and fermented veggies. I stock my cabinets with essentials to easily cook this type of food.

- Revisit historical knowledge about the role of children in social movements. Make sure that in addition to highlighting individual activists like Marley Dias, Naomi Wadler, Malala Yousafzai, and Greta Thunberg, you also explore the stories of young people who use collective power to make a difference.

- Teach children about historical heroes through story, play and books. Biographies are an amazing way to inspire children. Find biographies of young people doing social justice work, especially those living in your area.

- Point out racism or other isms when you see them happening. Talk openly about how you feel when observing.

- Find a school that has a curriculum which includes social justice. Surround yourself with a community who is justice-focused and active in that work.

- Let the kids in your life hear you talking, asking questions, and processing together.

- Share openly about why you make your choices. I speak to my kids about where I want to spend my money and whose pocket it will go into. They know about white men millionaires and what those men typically do with the wealth they've accumulated. I tell my children about how I want to spend our money to buy at local, BIPOC, women, or LGBTQIA+-owned businesses.

- Travel often, near and far, to see as many other ways of living as possible. Expose your children to other cultures and societies.

- Make friends with others who share your rhythms, even if that's just one or two families. You are more likely to celebrate new rituals if you have someone to support you and practice these rituals alongside you.

Invitations for Reflection

- What mantras do you personally use and want to teach to children?

- What rituals of mending and repairing do you use and want to teach to your community? If you don't have any yet, identify who around you engages in mending and repair. How can you learn from them?

- What marginalized voices do you need to listen to and invite into your life and community?

- What emotions are easiest for you to support? What emotions are the most triggering for you?

Chapter 7

Respect Nature

At Chavitos, teachers are called guides because we guide children through learning how to interact with the natural world around them. We believe if we teach younger generations the necessity of taking care of the earth, we can find a way for everyone to help in that endeavor and be conscious of their impact to avoid further climate crises. We teach children how to honor and respect nature through agreements we all share. Some of our agreements around this work are:

- Slow down and notice the breathtaking organisms and cycles happening around us.

- Take flowers and leaves that have already fallen to the floor. We want to respect the life cycle of all living things by not interrupting their growth and living cycle. Fallen flowers and leaves are plentiful and are an invitation to play while respecting nature.

- Climb sturdy trees with limbs wider than our arms. Healthy, thick branches can hold our weight and won't be snapped.

- Give gentle touches to insects, if any at all. It's better to use our eyes to observe the smaller organisms of our world than it is to use our hands. Smaller organisms are fragile and delicate.

- When harvesting, take what we need and leave the rest for animals we share our space with. Only harvest if there is plenty and if it's healthy for the organism to give to us.

- If picking things from trees or shrubs, pause and ask the flowers or grass if they want to be picked. We teach kids to listen to that voice inside of themselves, or their intuition, when harvesting the bounty of nature. We teach children that all organisms have a spirit and a will. It's our work to learn to listen. Kids often find listening to the plant's voices easier than listening to adults' voices.

- After harvesting, give something back. Sing a song, offer words of gratitude, pour fresh water, or sprinkle ash around the base of the organism we took from.

We have found that these agreements help us not to dominate nature, but to respect and collaborate with her. Children are naturally curious and can do these agreements better and more often than adults. However, it's a skill, just like learning empathy for others. Children need modeling on how to interact with nature in an honorable way. Guides model looking closely at nature with inquiry and curiosity.

To connect children to nature, we celebrate and follow Earth's cycles. We hold earth celebrations to honor what is happening on

Earth, rather than celebrations that revolve around materialism or consumerism. Solstices and Equinoxes, for example, are celebrated with guided meditations, singing, art, and puppet shows. Winter Solstice, in particular, is about the first day of winter and the sun returning. We celebrate it with homemade food, creating a spiral of cedar branches, lighting and tending a big fire, and gathering with songs and intentions about what is "rising" in our lives. We then use candles to celebrate the returning light on earth and our inner light. Nature celebrations are made with intention, are reflective and personal, and are regenerative and uplifting.

Another way we honor nature is by knowing what medicine is being offered in her soil. We learn the medicine of certain plants and then make medicine for the year together. Our activities are seasonal, and our food and medicine is seasonal when we honor and listen to the earth. We then create yearly rituals around foraging these seasonal foods. Our family knows early spring is time for nettles, dandelions, and maple flowers. In our cooking classes, we use chickweeds and purple dead nettle to make food. Our program rituals revolve around finding these plants, harvesting them, and using them dried or fresh. I use dried marigold flower petals to adorn a birthday cake in November. We drink lemon balm tea in class in summer. By learning the medicine offered by plants, children start to associate rituals with the food and medicine the earth provides.

Because we love the Earth, we also honor her by making conscientious lifestyle choices. We promote earth -friendly life-style practices to families in our communities, and we teach them to children in our program. There are the basics we all know: limit plastic, find doctors, dentists, and grocery stores close to your home, support local farmers markets, sign up for CSAs, invest in bikes and drive less. We also introduce other opportunities for conscientious choices to children, as well. For example, we learn about the horror of planting and harvesting palm oil and how it has overrun rainforests, with the focus of increasing profits instead of cultivating a supportive ecosystem. Our K-8 group looks at labels and refuses to buy products with palm oil ingredients. Students also know about earth advocates who lead protests to bring awareness to climate change, and they echo the words of Greta Thunberg, "You have stolen my dreams and my childhood with your empty words. And yet I'm one of the lucky ones. People are suffering. People are dying. Entire ecosystems are collapsing," she said. "We are in the beginning of a mass extinction, and all you can talk about is money and fairy tales of eternal economic growth. How dare you (Thunberg, 2019)." Matching her tenacity, passion and honesty, our students are impassioned by role models and a love for the Earth. They lead their own advocacy campaigns and spread awareness of current issues through their artwork and conversations. This passion from students naturally trickles down into their family systems, and gratefully, we see many simple earth-conscious habits being adapted by families in our community.

Another act of mindfulness that honors nature is to look at clothing labels and peek into your closets. I like to ask myself, where were my clothes made and by whom? What materials were used to make them? hat will happen to them after I'm done using them? Educate yourself on fast-fashion and the cost of inexpensive materials. One of my favorite books about this concept is   Fiber Shed by Rebecca Burgess with Courtney White (2019). Their mission is to support farmers, designers, and small brands as they reshape the textile industry through regional collaboration, ethical sourcing, and regenerative practices. They are proving that a sustainable future for fashion is already in motion. If you can, recalculate your spending and save money by buying less clothing of higher quality. I've tried to increase renewable resources into my clothing by buying hemp or merino wool clothing. I would rather have less clothes that can return to the earth instead of those that are filled with plastics and which engorge landfills when thrown out.

After being aware of what materials you are investing in, change your mindset around how to engage with the clothing, as well. Learn how to mend and repair. If your clothing gets holes in it, mend it or patch it, rather than donating or tossing it out. Luckily, right now there is a trend of visible mending, which is reducing the stigma around patches. In our community, we have cultivated a distaste for waste. We have students who come to school with patched knees, their repurposed socks become capes for their stuffed animals, and they hand their clothing down to others when they outgrow them. Together, we've created a school culture of fixing, mending, and repurposing items. We teach students the power behind simple acts of using a running stitch and regifting clothes. We see this lifestyle as a protest against consumerism. This lifestyle refuses the demand for constant consumerism. It helps us detach from the cycle of increasing consumption and instead connects us with regenerative practices that keep our dollars in our bank accounts, fabric out of landfills, and allows us to drive economy in other intentional ways.

This concept of reusing isn't new. All great ideas are inspired by the original creator: Earth. She herself is the master mender and radical reuser of waste. She did create mushrooms and molds, after all. I see her not wasting anything, but reclaiming it, recycling it, and redistributing it. When you see earth retraining a fallen tree to stretch high again, or a shell recalcifying, celebrate! Celebrate when one more piece of clothing, or tree, or branch, is given new life rather than tossed into an overflowing landfill or considered broken and useless. Nature finds a way to restore things and so can we. I'm grateful for this movement. And, luckily, there are a lot of resources surrounding this type of social activity, from in-person classes to books. My favorite book is *Mending Life: A Handbook for Repairing Clothes and Hearts Similarly*, written by Nina Montenegro and Sonya Montenegro.

Lastly, one of my favorite ways we can respect nature, and teach children to respect nature, is to follow her rhythms. We should mimic what she is doing in each season. In winter, should hibernate, go to bed early, and tend to the fireplace. In spring, eat your weeds to detox and revive your lymphatic system, adorn your home with flowers, and sprinkle local pollen on everything. Spark new dreams and plant baby seedlings, both in the physical soil and in your dream life. In summer, be active, stay up late, connect with others, bask in the sun, and eat wild berries full of antioxidants. If hot, soak in the local water. In the fall, be reflective and let go of habits and mindsets that don't serve you. Honor decomposition, stroll through changing forests and examine your relationship to change. Let practices that no longer bring you life die on the vine. By following the natural cycles around us, we will live more fulfilled, more nourished, and more aligned to earth, giving us more energy and focus. What are some habits you want to invite into your life in alignment to each unique season?

Behold the Spirit

One mindshift that helps us to engage with nature and to align with the above suggestions is to cultivate a sense of awe and reverence. Believe all living things are communicating with us with their unique energy radiating outward. If we are slow and attentive, like kids, we can tap into that life pulse and bow closer to learn more. If adults applied the same belief to our decision making, we'd be so much happier. We would be flooded with the wonderment that naturally shrouds children. What a good feeling that is.

An additional benefit to this connectedness is that it helps us make more informed decisions about our lives and the lives connected to ours.

The idea that all living beings and spiritual beings are connected and sacred is inescapably woven into our program agreements. We give permission and space for our children to listen to themselves and all living things by reminding them how to do it. We can do this by sharing stories of our personal processes, or including children in addressing problems and solutions related to upholding the sacred nature of all living things. We create space in our lessons that help children remember how to pay attention to small details around us that might just hold a message or key for us to unlock. Chavitos children and guides are taught to:

- Respect all plants, microorganisms, animals, and minerals in our shared space. This was their space first and we have just been granted permission to be in it. We observe how they are living and try to have the least amount of impact on them.

- Every part of the ecosystem has an essential and important purpose. No part is absolute. We respect the small and big parts of our ecosystem, knowing they're all interdependent.

- Just because we have the power to control something in our environment doesn't mean we should. Instead of trying to control something, we can consider how else can we engage with our environment without interrupting its purpose.

- We leave spaces as we find them. If we find a nest, instead of disturbing it, we consider how to observe it from a distance or simply not stress the foraging parents. We ask ourselves, *how can we coexist with things without changing their patterns or habits?*

- We honor the passing or death of another living being. Death is an important part of life. We don't need to be afraid of it. It is essential to make space for new life. We create ritual and honor emotions that rise when our beloved chickens die or when we witness a barn owl using its sharp beak to tear apart meat from a forest animal. Guides are taught to hold a sacred container for questions and observations about death. Guides teach that emotions have space and are welcome when processing.

- Children need autonomy. We guide children through the implications of their choices at all ages.

Appreciate Beauty Alongside Functionality

Nature makes the most breathtaking and beautiful things. She stops us in our tracks. Our human brains are drawn to her balance, symmetry, and the intentional functionality she imbues in all she makes. The colors she weaves together draw us and pollinators to the flowers, promising future fruit. We should let nature's beauty draw us toward it, and include those elements of beauty, in small and big details, within our programs. A question we ask as program administrators is, *how do we share this truth and teach this to children?* Ways we can do so include the following:

- We provide high quality materials and tools that withstand intense usage. We ensure our tools are made of natural materials and can be fixed or repurposed if broken. We are mindful about not filling our spaces with low quality tools made of thin plastic. These break easily and can't be fixed.

- We mend tools when broken. Felt, wood, and metal can be reconnected and given new life. For things that can't be fixed, if they are made of natural materials, we allow them to return to the earth.

- We model how to fix things. We ask children to help reconnect a shovel's handles, reattach a wagon wheel, or mend a hole in their winter hat.

- We expect children to clean up their spaces after snacking, playing, and classes. Chavitos spaces are shared spaces with animals and plants, so we consider the effects of our actions, big or small. This might include asking a child to think about the impact of a gum wrapper on the floor and what might happen if a curious chicken is drawn to the sparkle of the wrapper. Additionally, we teach children that each shovel and basket of crayons has a specific place on the shelf. Just like with nature, our spaces have order (think about cup nests, lines of sedimentary sand, and tree rings). Order feels good for our nervous system because it gives us certainty and fulfills our expectations. We know where to find our materials when we store them correctly, in the right places. We return items to their rightful places for ease and flow of future lessons. When supplies are not in the right place, we waste time hunting for them. When our spaces are tidy and our things are put away in the right places, we feel pride and connection to them, and the environment, and we are more likely to care for them.

The material of toys makes a difference in how a child interacts with it. We can ground our play with natural materials. Natural toys are the perfect example of the marriage of beauty and multifunctionality. Natural wood, felts, and fabrics all have an energy that soothes and connects us to the earth and its cycles. These materials feel solid and good in our hands. I find their natural patterns or texture connects me to the process of how it was whittled or woven. Everything living and non-living has an imprint, a story. And if we're listening, we can hear those stories.

Natural materials and their simplicity also offer ample opportunities for creativity and imagination. Their open-endedness leads users to change or shift play depending on where their motivation strikes. This is where nature is at its best. Nature has scattered play material and invitations to play all over the earth: stones, logs, sticks, flowers, leaves, roots, dirt, clay, wind, and rain. These are all wonderful materials and tools that have countless possibilities for children engaged in play. A stone can be stacked to create a decorative tower, lined up to define a pathway leading to a fairy house, clinked together with other stones to create music, or hold a beat in a song. They can be hidden and found or used to grind petals or dirt. I love using a sharp stone to loosen another rock or cut a vine. In our classes, I've seen rocks collected in a pile, shined, washed, lined up, tossed into an empty space, gathered in a bowl for a mud kitchen meal, or hidden and found again. Those needing sensory input can heave and pile a heavy bucket of stones using their lifting muscles. Those needing calm play can dunk stones in water and observe their color changing. Our natural materials meet all children where they are at and fulfill multiple needs. You can probably list at least 10 more things to do with stones that I've not thought of. Limitless opportunities and invitations exist with this simple, sturdy earth material.

There is something so satisfying about playing with nature's tools. Our bodies remember the tools of our ancestors: a fabric handkerchief, a whittled digging tool, a heated cooking element, a bone game token. Nature's tools are also free and widely available. Utilizing free and natural materials is a great way to fight and resist the corporate agenda of consumerism. Obviously, playing with free toys which grow with a child doesn't meet the motivations of corporations who are often fueled by greed. It's a radical choice to add beauty and multifunctionality into your play by using natural objects. It's radical to be mindful about what toys and materials you bring into the classroom or home. No need to pull out your pocketbook and spend money on a toy that will keep your child's attention for a mere few months.

I had to be incredibly intentional to get my own family out of a cycle of over consumption. I grew up with an overflowing Christmas tree, with countless, beautifully wrapped gifts underneath it. Jose didn't grow up with many toys or possessions, so I had easeful support from him when we decided, as a family, to reduce our consumption. It was easy for our family to start a new Christmas tradition. We decided to buy one gift for Christmas and one gift for each of our birthdays, which are all in January. Even better if that one gift was an experience. We wanted to teach our own children, at a young age, how experiences could also be gifts. If we gift an experience, we create memories together, which long outlast a toy. These changes around gifting during celebrations honor beauty and multifunctionality in a different way. Now, at eleven years old, my oldest declares often, "I'd rather travel than get a gift."

The more difficult part of reducing our consumption was changing our extended families' expectations. This did happen though, through multiple conversations and practice. Instead of holding traditional American Christmas celebrations each year, we now visit Rio Dulce or Antigua with our Guatemalan family. When we do, we give a family member a night in a hotel as our Christmas gift. Gradually, this has become more of a norm, and now, our Guatemalan cousins request an adventure for their birthdays rather than the traditional piñata and party with frosted cake and soda. It has been amazing to see that transition.

When our purchases inside the home and classroom have intentionality woven into them, they improve our spaces and our overarching lives. We practice this mindfulness by asking the following questions before bringing new tools into our spaces:

- Is this beautiful and naturally made?
- Where were the materials sourced from?
- Who made this? Were they paid a living and fair wage?
- Will this tool grow with the kids? Can they use this when they're two years old? What about when they're ten years old?
- Does this have multiple purposes? Can it be used for many different things?
- Is there something in nature that can serve the same purpose?
- Can I find this tool for free somewhere else? Do I or someone in the community already have this? If not, can I source it for free?
- What is the best way to store this so its beauty is honored and it is used often?

Just like in nature, we can bring beauty and intention into our homes and programs. We can buy less and more high-quality products by asking ourselves questions like these and being intentional with our choices.

Invitations for Reflection

- What procedures and agreements can you add to your program that will increase beauty and wonder?

- Is there an area in your space that is an eye-sore? If so, brainstorm three ways you can transform it. What would you replace? What would you add?

- To increase your awareness of all that "glimmers," start a daily routine of writing down a moment or interaction that made you happy during your day and was filled with spirit.

Chapter 8

Teach Outdoors

There are many names for nature: Mother Earth, Turtle Island, Mama Gaia. The one I use most in our family and community is Gaia. I am absolutely in love with Gaia and have been my whole life, starting when I wore moon boots in a mud puddle as a toddler. I love deeply observing Gaia. She has solutions for every problem we create. She covers bare soil to keep it from eroding. She creates cycles of balance to keep populations under control. She invented symmetry, scent, and patterns to attract and populate. And she celebrates queerness.

Humanity's lack of observation of Gaia has created imbalance. But one thing I know is if there is a problem with our surroundings, it's because there is an imbalance somewhere. If we watch and see how Gaia responds, we can learn the solution to those problems. Therefore, we should consider her the ultimate teacher. Hands down, Gaia teaches life lessons better than any other guide could. Our human teachers are guides who direct a child to look to her for answers and inspiration.

There are countless life lessons within nature. In permaculture, they say, you don't have a slug problem, you have a duck problem. In a similar vein, Gaia will show us what is missing from our (eco)systems and will show us how it can be fixed if we focus and connect with her. In spring, we see dandelions, chick weed, purple dead nettle, stinging nettle, miner's lettuce, and all sorts of "weeds" growing. They all grow at the perfect time to wake a hibernating body, to clear the fats we need during the slow winter, and to stimulate natural detoxing. If we pay attention and are aligned to these cycles, we can find natural solutions to our problems right under our feet. In this way, we must embrace the weeds instead of poisoning them and listen to their wisdom, which is readily available.

Chavitos programs are outdoors for all these reasons and more. We are outdoors because the outdoors offers the most enriched environment our children have access to. There, we find examples of resilience, balance, abundance, and artistry in every leaf, branch, and rock. Nature invites all our senses into teaching and learning. When we engage our senses, we can feel the rhythm of the earth pulsing around us, and we are called to explore and be creative in our endeavors to learn. Smells waft from lilies and make us stop to breathe deeply, filling our lungs. Buzzing bees alert us to some busy work happening nearby that benefits our community. A sting from an ant bite tells us we're invading someone else's space. A bitter berry tells us to wait, it's too early to enjoy their bounty. Everything is ready according to its own time.

When kids play in nature, and most of their time is spent outside, they're more aware of nature's solutions to problems. They learn about life cycles, and that everything has purpose, even in death. This is an especially important component of learning for children in American culture, where we don't talk about death and we lack rituals surrounding grief. Where else, besides nature, will our children learn about or see examples of the

life cycle? A good example of this can be seen on our farm, where wild
rabbits eat the lettuce we grow. It's common for those rabbits to also get
eaten by coyotes. As students and guides walk on our farm, we sometimes
see rabbits' body parts left behind by coyotes, and that's okay. The scene
is a reminder that everything has a purpose. The rabbit, the coyote, the
lettuce, the farmer… no entity is evil or bad for its participation in the
life cycle. This lesson, that everything has a purpose, is comforting in a
world that grows increasingly unfair and where only a few in the dominant
culture hold the power that affects the remaining majority. I appreciate that
Gaia offers constant reminders that there is a natural cycle, a purpose, a
reason, for everything here on earth. Nature can and will correct us. When
Chavitos students spend most of their time outdoors, we see this lesson, and
many more, played out on a micro-scale, but with global players. Rabbits,
coyotes, eagles, field mice, and other animals know no boundaries. Sure,
we see and interact with them on our two acres of farmland, but animals
are not beholden to our fences or deeds. They are global inhabitants of
the earth. We can erect a fence, but animals will always remind us of the
folly of doing so.

By spending our days outside, our classroom is expanded to include
all the lessons nature has to offer. Our preschool program is fully outdoors.
Children who attend preschool there spend three hours in the open air,
under a lush tree canopy. Our K-8 program offers five out of six hours of
instruction outdoors. The remaining hour is spent in either a geodome,
open-aired gazebo, or a rustic, three-walled classroom space that opens
to the farm. Remaining connected to the earth during our schooldays
fulfills a basic human need to be part of the natural world. Remaining
connected allows us to feel the earth's moods, seasons, ailments and
abundance. With that connection, we can better learn from and address
the needs of the earth. This is a kind of recalibration process that re-centers

Mama Gaia as the teacher and adult educators as guides connecting students to her wonder.

When children spend extended time in nature, we cultivate hope for our earth within them. As adults, we might have become disconnected from earth as living beings. This makes it easier to ignore the hurt we inflict on earth from our choices and the lasting impact our choices have on our ecosystems. Let's take the monarch butterfly as an example. The mere existence of monarch butterflies benefits and impacts an extensive range of plants and animal ecosystems. If children know the monarch butterfly individually, if they have personal connections to the butterfly (which they were able to cultivate in their childhood by spending time outdoors), they might grow into adults who make decisions that positively impact the butterfly, which is a keystone species. But if we overschedule our kids, keep them indoors instead of outdoors, and limit their opportunities to engage with nature, they won't know how to preserve or value nature as adults. They won't develop personal or lasting connections to other creatures. They may not learn to advocate for other species or the general preservation of nature in their adulthood. This is why it is so important to offer our children nature-based education that allows them to spend a significant amount of time outdoors, in direct connection with nature. We must help children learn, from a young age, how to tend and care for her.

Being outside in all weather is also healthy for our bodies. Our bodies are made to move and absorb the microbes in the dirt. Our eyes need to focus on distant objects to balance out the short-distance sight we over-engage in with screen use. Our internal rhythms and nervous system need opportunities to slow down, and calm down, after being over-stimulated in society and social interactions. Nature offers us opportunities to slow down and resettle. When we are immersed in nature, our heart rate, blood pressure, and cortisol levels naturally reduce to healthier levels. We also shed fear and stress when in nature, which allows us to better relax and rest. Engaging with nature is a way for us to naturally disengage from our endless hustle and bustle. At our forest location, it's common for students and guides to crouch down to look at a wiggly worm or crane our necks to watch the flickers feeding their babies in the treetops. Doing so helps us to engage in a wide range of movement and motion. Our bodies and all muscle groups are engaged and stimulated.

To make extended time outdoors a positive and fruitful experience in our programs, there are a few practices we engage in:

1. We support parents by having a detailed and specific list of required clothing. We list brands and types of clothing. We specify which items need hook and loop straps to tighten around wrists and ankles, and remind parents that clothing should not have bobbles or decorative elements on them (so clothing stays put and dry when it rains).

2. We have a gear check at the beginning of the year to make sure each family has the correct supplies. We check waterproofness and report back to parents with any requests to change gear.

3. We have a collection of lendable gear for families to check out. Kids grow fast, and by sharing clothing that no longer serves one child, but could serve another, we support the earth and resist fast-fashion.

4. We teach families about layering and use pictures to support the process.

5. When hiring, we ask for a recent story about an outdoor adventure to see if the outdoors is indeed a central and comfortable part of someone's life. We make sure guides have the correct gear and mindset about "all weather."

6. We ask guides to model bliss in all types of weather and acknowledge the lessons we can take from each season. We say, "Let's lay on our backs and watch the raindrop fall," not "Yuck, rain!" or "This is good weather for being inside, reading a book."

7. Our guides must have tools and strategies for keeping kids warm when kids have trouble self-regulating their temperature needs. Guides should know the signs of a cold or hot child and encourage removing or adding a layer when necessary. They should invite students to play a running game to warm up or an activity in the shade to cool down.

After spending time in a multisensory classroom of nature, the dim and synthetic rhythms of the classroom may be boring for children. Humans are the center of this synthetic environment. The heartbeat is measured, metered, and finite. The classroom only allows us to focus on one thing at a time and it cuts out so many opportunities for learning. It is so controlled that we don't engage many parts of our brains while we are there. I've observed this in my classroom and others. Recently, I heard from a kindergarten teacher whose classroom looked out into a beautiful courtyard with garden beds and a painted mural labyrinth. I was one of the teachers who helped make intentional decisions about how this school was built, and how to include movement invitations between the indoor and outdoor spaces. I was so saddened to hear of a student's experience in that classroom: the blinds were always drawn so students wouldn't be distracted by the outdoors. I thought about children who often look like they are daydreaming but are deeply processing some aspect of their life. Why not open the windows and doors and use that labyrinth in the courtyard as an invitation between work cycles? Why not let those children move and meditate, to process and learn? Our bodies don't know how to handle all the control that classrooms, and other human-centered spaces, exert on us.

We think we learn best in controlled environments like this, but that is a misconception.

Conversely, when we learn to exist as part of a wider ecosystem, like that of Mother Nature, we begin to understand that Gaia's intention is for everything to be well and whole. The earth is here to support and love us. She has all her babies' well-being in mind, from the smallest sapling to the largest oak tree to human beings. Even things that seem devastating to humans, like volcanoes and natural fires, bring balance back to the earth, which is a form of medicine at the planetary level. We need to teach our children to be aware of, and to respect and carry forward, this wisdom and balance that mother earth demonstrates. Perhaps the laws our children create, as a result, will be more holistic. Wise leaders return to mother earth for their solutions. They gravitate toward solutions that benefit multiple groups of people. They base their decisions on what the global majority needs. When children are connected to Gaia, their decisions will come from a place that considers value beyond what we humans bring. They will know their impact is expansive and will slow down to include and be mindful of all elements involved.

Recently, during a literacy class, I was reading aloud about geese. At that exact moment, geese flew over our farm, adding the perfect sound effect to the book! We were all in shock and the children squealed with glee. I paused the lesson as the children naturally flocked to the huge geodome window. Some ran outside. When I let wonder take over a lesson like this, magical learning happens. If I had tried to control the moment or ignored the geese flying overhead, we would have missed out on holistic learning. Instead, the students now know what geese honking really sounds like and when reading about them in the future, that real sound effect will be in their head rather than my imitation of them.

Invitations for Reflection

- What is your current relationship with nature? Is there a habit you want to start or improve?

- When children see you, will they see you comfortably embracing all weather?

- What is the most recent nature experience you've had? What was your level of enjoyment? Do your personal experiences demonstrate a high level of comfort and pleasure from nature?

- What percentage of time do you want your nature program to be held outdoors? If your answer is less than 70%, who can support you to offer more time outdoors?

Chapter 9
Offer Unstructured Play

I have always known I want to reclaim play for the generations of children who come after me. Unstructured play, particularly, is important for the emotional development of all kids, at all ages. Unstructured play is a timeframe in which no one is leading a child in an activity or lesson. During this time, students get to decide what they do. Unstructured play allows children to drop into a mental and emotional state in which they can process what they see, hear, and feel in the world. They might incorporate things from movies they've watched, feelings they're having, and conversations they overheard. Allowing children this freedom helps them to build their executive function and teaches them to listen to their bodies, their needs, and their desires. It helps children learn the appropriate time to act upon those needs and desires, too.

Unstructured play is one of the cornerstones of the Chavitos preschool framework, and it is also an important part of our K-8 program. Organizationally, we believe all ages of children learn faster through play, laughter and games. Our brains seek patterns that are often built into children's games. Our bodies naturally gravitate toward activities and work that games instigate, and we are hardwired with curiosity. Unfortunately, this sacred time of unstructured play is becoming less prevalent for children as they grow. Their days become more planned and scheduled the older they get. Schools, and our culture, expect kids to grow up too quickly. We reduce or take away opportunities for play far too early. As a result, children miss out on learning opportunities they would only be exposed to because of play.

To counter that level of regulation, we ensure kids at Chavitos get to enjoy long stretches of unstructured play. We do so by building time frames of unstructured play into their schedules. At our forest preschool, all classes are unstructured. At our K-8 farm, there are designated times for movement and unstructured play. In both programs, unstructured time is an essential part of our daily rhythm.

Because everyone's energy and needs are different and will change throughout the day, unstructured play can look very different. Sometimes, students come to school tired, so they choose to sit in the sand pit or put their feet into the water feature area. Or maybe a student is bursting with energy and wants to connect with their friends, so they invite others to play games and run through the corn maze or vegetable rows, or to hide under the cedar boughs. Forms of unstructured play we witness children engaged in within learning spaces at Chavitos include:

- Chasing each other through corn and vegetable rows
- Using loose building materials and tool parts to create games based on books
- Hiding and finding beanbags or glass jewels
- Collecting dirt and shifting sand in the mud kitchen
- Making forts from blankets and sheets using bamboo poles

- Pulling each other in wagons
- Soccer and hockey on a deck using feet
- Building with Brain Flakes, blocks, and dominoes
- Playing chess
- Chipping rocks to find gems inside or just to make them crumble
- Using magnifying glasses to create sunbeams and smoke
- Deseeding sunflower seeds and sucking on them, scattering them to the chickens, or saving the seeds for next season

To encourage unstructured play, we have a lot of loose parts or materials available to children in our programs. These tools can be transformed into many different things when a child's imagination takes over. Some of our favorite loose materials are:

Crates	Tires	Flower Petals
Buckets	Pillows	Water
Ropes	Sheets	Logs
Pulleys	Wood shavings	Gutters
Pipes		

Extended amounts of time engaged in unstructured play allows children to benefit from the flow factor, or the feeling of engaging in an activity so deeply that they forget about the world around them. We sometimes call this deep play. Deep play and the flow factor are achieved by not having an agenda or a schedule for young learners ages two through five-years-old. The forest naturally provides children with invitations to enter deep play. At our forest location, there is a sandpit that has metal cake molds, handled shifts, and scoops that children love to play with. Our guides often leave the sandpit open for children to enter, and those same children often end up staying there for the whole class. Deep play might also look like a child just scooping and dumping sand repetitively. While this might seem simple, at first, there is a lot more going on than meets the eye: the child is observing volume; they are learning about cause and effect when a vessel is filled; they're gaining sensory input of different textures of wet and dry sand. Deep play is the vessel that leads them toward these scientific discoveries.

Children test what they learn over and over. This is exploration. It is crucial that we leave room for children to play in curious and exploratory ways because without an agenda, task, or a stated expectation of learning, a child will organically learn what their brain and hands are ready to absorb. This exploration is the best example of how children naturally learn. Furthermore, exploration doesn't need to be taught to them. We humans are all born with the instinct to explore. It's our job, as adults, to create an environment that draws this out, inspires interaction, and invites exploration.

Play is the way in which children naturally learn, and they learn by using their hands. Their fingers are strengthened by the gripping of shovel handles, or the pinching of a pine needle, or pulling flower petals from the steeples. Their fingers build strength by engaging in play like this. Someday, when they are six or seven years old, they will be ready to grip a pencil to write their name on a paper. The path toward that future is paved through play.

Social and Moral Intelligence

Play also teaches social and moral intelligence skills. Social intelligence is based on soft skills that are connected to one's spirit and heart. They include compassion, grit, sympathy, problem-solving, conflict management, and communicating feelings. Moral intelligence is about being connected to our conscience, about how we believe people should be treated. Kindness, justice, fairness, and equality fall into this category. Social and moral intelligence skills are hard to measure, hard to test for, and historically, schools don't spend time, energy, or money on them. At Chavitos, we believe teaching these skills is essential to raising well-rounded children. We believe in the following social and moral intelligences:

- Everyone is valuable. Everyone has the right to take up space and to use their voice to advocate for what they need. Children have rights and adults listen and honor these rights.

- Everyone's opinion is important. We share our opinions about how we want to do something, and then as a group, we decide what works best. Students decide for themselves what roles they want to play when engaged in games and play.

- We ask and give consent. Everyone has a chance to give consent. When using a material, we are asked if we want to share. We are asked permission to hug or invited to run. If we don't want to play in a certain way, we do not have to consent. We voice our consent or lack thereof.

- Everyone listens to their bodies and shares what they need. Children can decide how many layers they want or don't want to wear. We listen to children's needs and recognize their needs might be different from ours.

CASE STUDY

Play naturally creates opportunities for children to build these social and moral intelligences. For instance, play gives us opportunities to solve problems when a ball goes over the neighbor's fence. This happened when my children were younger and were playing in a small group. I stood back and watched the children brainstorm different ways to get the ball back. As they tried different solutions, including using a stick to get the ball back and trying to reach under the fence with their hands, I was struck by their ability to listen to all ideas and try out the ones they thought were best. After trying many different solutions, they were successful in getting their ball back. They'd used a stick, rope, ladder, and bucket. Once they got the ball back, they cheered and celebrated so loudly it was as if their favorite soccer team had won the World Cup! Unstructured play held the space for these kids to take as much time as they needed to solve problems. All the play they had engaged in over the years as students in our school came in handy when they thought through which materials could be used in different ways to get their ball back. Play led them to think outside the box and creatively find ways to use the materials they had on hand.

Play also naturally brings up power dynamics. Learning how to recognize, address, and wield power is a moral intelligence. If children can learn how to share power and how to be aware of those who are lacking power in a game, then we will eventually have adults in power who do the same. But, getting to that reality starts with the invitation to play, with ladders and wagons when we are kids, and eventually, laws and business models when we are adults.

Invitations for Reflection

- What percentage of your time within your day is intentionally unstructured? How can you build unstructured time into your schedule?

- How do you want to incorporate unstructured time into your nature school program? Where and when in the daily rhythms will you include it?

- Do you have a "loose parts" area in your nature school program space? What types of supplies and materials do you want to add to that space?

Chapter 10
Accept Risky Play

Outside, while engaged in unstructured play, children are given opportunities to try things they're uncomfortable doing. Things like climbing a tree, swinging, balancing on a log, picking up a big stick, walking on unstable surfaces, or being near a fire. We call this "risky play." Risky play is great for children, as it presents situations they'd otherwise be kept from participating in despite the relative safety involved. It's typical nowadays for parents in our culture to hover over their children, trying their best to protect and prevent accidents. But our children are not benefiting from all this overzealous attention to safety. They need exposure to controlled risk-taking experiences, which is exactly what risky play is.

Nature offers invitations to risky play. Through nature, children can come to know and learn about their bodies. When engaged in risky play, they are pushed to an edge, and it's there, at that moment, when they learn to listen to their bodies and their messages. If a child is really scared, they might want to get down from the tree they're climbing. So, as guides in the forest and on the farm, we encourage children to do that, and then to return to the activity later. Another good example is a ladder leaning against an apple tree in our orchard. Sometimes, kids get up the ladder but then have trouble getting down. When this happens, we guide them down one branch, one foot, at a time. We never lift them down. Our guidance might sound like this,

> "Put your foot lower.
> Great, now move your hands to a lower branch.
> You're almost there!"

When we guide children through risky activities like this, over time (often not much more than a few weeks), they learn they can, in fact, safely participate in things that scare them and they can accomplish risky feats. There's a lot of confidence-building and celebration for kids engaged in risky play. Furthermore, guiding children through risky play transfers to activities at home, like climbing bunk beds. Risky play allows kids to learn they can do hard things they might initially think are impossible.

As adults, we engage in risky play all the time, in both physical and emotional ways. We cook over fire, use a chainsaw to remove a fallen tree from a path, climb up ladders to clean off a roof, walk on that roof to fix a gutter, ski down alpine slopes, hike with bears and moose, play the stock market, work towards a degree while working and raising kids… Obviously, some adults are more prone to risk while others seek the comfort of home and the ground. But I'm sure we can all identify ways we've taken risks. Taking risks teaches kids to listen to their intuition (which is often silenced in our culture) and over time, the importance of discernment. Discernment is being attuned to our animal bodies. Our animal bodies feel joy, anger, and other basic feelings that give us important information. This is an important lesson children need to learn when they're young so they can navigate their chosen paths later, as adults.

At the farm and forest, we see children sit back and observe before they take risks. They will do this for days, weeks, even months… thinking about an activity. Eventually, they'll try it out. This internal process is one our society doesn't honor or validate because we're too focused on data. But it's an important process for children to go through. They need to build intuitive muscles. They need to listen to that little voice in their mind and body. They need to believe their voices, and choices, are valid. We are also teaching children that they can do hard things, as Glennon Doyle asserts in her book, *Untamed* (Dial Press, 2020). We are teaching kids they have support with guides, peers, and parents. Over time, kids will build a library of positive risk association memories. This is why risk isn't inherently bad. It teaches us important things about ourselves.

Even as an adult, I still must practice discernment and intuitive decision making all the time. I must remind myself that my process, however long or short, is valid. As adults, we need to listen to our intuition for longer periods, and more often. We can strengthen this by doing things as simple as feeling cold and then putting on another layer. We can't plan for everything that might happen in life, which is why we need to listen to our inner voice and let it guide us on our journey.

Guides and parents must be prepared to dive into modeling and helping children listen to their intuitive muscles. Guides might hear, "I want my parents!" from a student and need to quickly connect the dots between what that child is saying and what that child's body is telling them. Is their body shivering? Perhaps the underlying need behind "I need my parents!" is actually another layer of clothes, not the presence of a parent. Risky play opens-up dialogue between children and guides that children need to have internally. However, this must be modeled to them externally, at first, because they don't necessarily know how to listen to their bodies yet.

Chavitos guides have dialogue with children that reflect the child's emotions back to them. Imagine seeing a young child shaking and saying, "Pick me up!" while on the rung of a ladder, no longer actually climbing up it. Instead of picking them up, a guide would say,

"I see your legs are shaking out of exertion. How are you feeling? What do you think you need to do?"

"Pick me up, pick me up!" the child might repeat.

"You're scared. But you can do hard things one step at a time. Try the left foot first…"

Step by step, the guide would talk the child down the ladder without physically helping them down.

If we prevent children from engaging in risky play — "careful, you're going too high." — when we take them off the ladder, or rescue them from the branch, we're curtailing their learning practice. The child is robbed of the joy of the accomplishment. We do this often in our society. Parents are prone to sweeping in and cleaning the mess or taking a child off the ledge. As parents, we think of all the things that could happen. But usually, those things don't happen. And if we step in, we rob children of a confidence-building opportunity. We miss the magic of seeing a child get down from a place that was hard to get to when they didn't think they could do it.

Another method of guiding children through risky play is to remind them about safety agreements. Let's use an example of a conversation between a child and a guide during risky play. Let's assume a child is on the tree and is unsure of what to do next. We begin with questions and comments that might include,

"Is the tree sturdy? Check the branch to make sure it's strong and can hold weight. Step on it."

"Wet branches can be slippery."

"How does your body feel?"

The conversation may progress to directly address the emotional state of the child, instead of the physical.

"I'm scared!" the child might say.

"It's okay to be scared! What are you going to do?" we can respond instead of saying, "Careful!" Or we can try a different tactic.

"I'm here for support. Look around you, what do you need to climb higher?"

We can also offer our own noticings to a child who might have tunnel vision because of fear or trepidation.

"I'm noticing that when it rains, the tree is slippery. What do you notice about wet surfaces? How do you want to climb that tree?"

"It's wet! My boot keeps slipping," children tend to respond.

As guides, we should ask children questions to help them identify what is dangerous around them. We get them to notice. This is inquiry-based instruction. Over time, it will lead to children learning independently. If we start this at age two, we see that by age ten, we hardly have any safety issues with children because they are aware (and have been, for many years) of safety and danger concerns.

"Big stick, big space," is a phrase we use at our farm and forest all the time. It is a great example of one lesson that leads to many lessons, to extended and independent learning. It teaches children that big tools require big spaces, and it reinforces that attempting to use big tools in small spaces leads to danger. In a similar way, we teach kids that we don't raise a shovel over our head just like we wouldn't raise a stick over our head. This is how children learn about body orientation and spatial awareness. They learn not to bump their bodies into other bodies, especially when engaging with large objects.

The practice of addressing risk and accepting risky play looks different each time we engage with it. Sometimes, it looks like a child jumping off a tree stump. Other times, it looks like them speaking up with a differing opinion during a group project. As adults, it can also look like addressing an ongoing problem with your life partner. The point is, if we start teaching children about risk awareness when they're young, they learn the skills they need to follow their intuition, listen to their body, and take calculated risks throughout their lifetime. That is how risky play unfolds over time. It's also a good framework for learning to honor agreements and boundaries of those involved in our lives, even if the world is operating on other agreements. When we are a part of a community, one that is dedicated to honoring each other, we can engage in taking calculated risks and trusting ourselves within those risks. Our interactions can then be less about placing fear and distrust on our children and more about being in the moment with our children and having beautiful, supportive interactions with them.

Invitations for Reflection

- What is your personal relationship to risk? Are you a daredevil tempting fate or a comfort seeker looking for retreat?

- Become aware of how your personal relationship to fear impacts others. Do you accept others' level of risk? Do you hear yourself repeating phrases that limit or ignore risk?

- What are some mantras you want to adopt and try out regarding risky play?

Chapter 11
Welcome Conflict

Conflict is an important part of life. It's a peak experience, and it is an attempt at connection. This is why we believe deeply that children must learn to be in conflict. Learning to stand in conflict helps children become boundary setters, clear communicators connected to the heart, thoughtful menders, and to take responsibility for their choices and how they affect others. At Chavitos, we value and normalize conflict. We make space for it when it shows up. We look it straight in the eye and say, *hello. I see you. What are you trying to show me?*

When it comes to conflict, we need to teach children how to process in a way that does not hurt others. Conflict shows us where we have room to realign our actual behaviors with those we wish to embody, and which are aligned with the values we hold. If we want and expect a certain behavior from children, we must teach it explicitly, model it in action, and then gradually release responsibility to the child until they reach independence. When I see children in conflict, I ask them simple questions to help them reflect.

"What happened? You look so sad?"

"How do you think _____ was feeling?"

"What do you need?"

Eventually, children will ask these questions themselves without being prompted, but at first, they need to be modeled to them. After a child has calmed down, they tend to think through these questions while engaged in play or by repeating and retelling the story of what happened. This is healthy and it moves the emotion from the feeling part of the brain to the logical part of the brain. This is explained by Dan Siegel and Tina Payne Bryson in their books <u>The Whole Brain Child (2011)</u> and <u>The Yes Brain (2018).</u> In The Whole Brain Child, Dr. Siegel writes,

> *"Sometimes parents avoid talking about upsetting experiences, thinking that doing so will reinforce their children's pain or make things worse. Actually, telling the story is often exactly what children need, both to make sense of the event and to move on to a place where they can feel better about what happened."*

Play is the stage where children process emotions and events. Because kids need to process by retelling or reenacting the story, we shouldn't attempt to control their play or the number of times they retell the story. Storytelling is how they share and get understanding around an event. Kids need to be able to play and experiment with acting out the things they see around them. This is how they learn to safely process what they experience.

While some children process conflict, we may see them stuck in a victim mindset. When my youngest child demonstrates this, or talks about feeling alone, feeling like power is being used against them, feeling helpless or despair, or having loss of vision, I simply ask them if they are stuck. They can quickly identify if they are or are not. Then, we work together to get them unstuck and back into alignment with their natural state of being.

Over time, they learned to ask for help, support, and compassion from people they trust. Having and using a curriculum about conflict also helps our students build language around their experiences. They can identify big emotions of helplessness and despair, and then they can feel empowered to voice and shift those feelings out.

Occasionally, we must also allow our children to go past the boundary line they, or we, hold with each other. At times, we only learn a lesson when we pass a boundary and are confronted with the conflict that arises as a result from that crossing. This is also how we, as parents, learn about the practices and techniques we may have learned and carry with us into our parenting, but which do not serve us or our children. We might overreact to something our child does or react so strongly that our children are affected by it, and then realize we still carry wounds around those topics from our own childhood. Once we see those behaviors or ideas at play in our own parenting, we can better assess where/what they are rooted in, whether they are necessary in the dynamic with our own children, whether we want to carry them forward with us, or whether we want to lay them down and move away from them.

We can begin to normalize conflict when our children are young by mirroring and putting words to what children do. Remember, we must model the behaviors and language we want our children to adopt. We should start by saying what we didn't like and then expressing what we want to happen. Eventually, children will learn to do this on their own. Here's an example of this kind of modeling, which normalizes conflict and making clear requests: "I didn't like how you jumped on my back without asking me. Can you ask me next time before you jump on my back?"

When we model conflict, it encourages us, as parents, to pause and relay to children what is happening inside our bodies, minds, and spirits. The trick is to pause first, and reflect, because the brain can't necessarily interpret the scenario when we are triggered by conflict. We need to regain calm first by pausing. Imagine a scenario where a child breaks a parent's earring while playing in the parent's bedroom.

"I'm feeling big emotions of disappointment and judgment. I need to take some space," we can say.

Then, we can return to the situation after we've regained our composure and share our reflection.

"When I saw my earring break, I felt disappointed."

Next, we use our words to set boundaries.

"You are not invited to my room because I want my possessions kept whole."

Once we set a boundary, we model it. The next day, when the same child wants to rest on the parent's bed, we might say,

"Please leave my room, I'm worried my things will get broken. We can revisit this when I see you respecting my things."

Lastly, we can model and start the mending process.

"Would you like to talk more about this?... I'm sad my earring was broken... What happened (Pause for their response)? Is there a way you can fix this and make it right with me?"

Listen to their ideas and decide on one together.

"I get it. You were angry about your brother teasing you."

"What can you do instead of breaking my things?" This puts the responsibility of finding alternative solutions back on the child.

"Let's try spending time in my room with me for a bit."

And when we see new behavior, we want to reinforce, acknowledge it.

"Oh, I love how gentle you are with the pillows on my bed."

Mending can be tricky because a lot of adults never learned how to mend and repair. When I went to school, there weren't any lessons around moral intelligence and it wasn't explicitly taught in my childhood home, either. Heck, some of us have never learned how to communicate problems and conflict in a healthy way. That's okay. It's great to be aware of and honest with where we are starting. There is no shame in not knowing how to do this. Our kids can see through us when we are trying to fake our way through something, so it's important to be honest with them about our process and how we are growing. Learning to do this, and communicating that effort to your children, is not only important for our children, but for ourselves, as well. And we are more than capable of teaching ourselves to do this. We can learn conflict and repair skills. We can find resolutions that work for all parties. To bring about a brighter future, our children need to learn how the process looks and feels. They should be aware, from a very young age, that finding resolution and repairing feels different in our bodies than if we stuff, ignore, or run away from our conflicts, thus preventing repair, connection, and the growth it brings.

Addressing, moving through, and learning to find resolution and repair is not a linear process. Sometimes you must go in a loop or backtrack to a previous stage before you can come out the other side. Sometimes, I find I'm ready to repair with a child, but they aren't yet. Or they are ready, and I'm not calm yet. It's okay if both parties aren't on the same timeline for mending. It is, however, important to communicate kindly where we are at. That might look and sound like you, the adult, saying,

"I need a little more time to process," or "I need some space, please," or "I'm still thinking about what happened and I'm not ready to talk yet. I'll let you know when I am."
When both people are ready, start the check-in process for mending. That might sound like,

"Are you ready for me to make it right?"

"That was intense. Are you ready to talk about what happened?"

"I can see you are calmer. I feel steady, too. Want to talk?"

"I made you mad, what did I do?"

As we've all witnessed with ourselves and other humans, if our children's emotional needs are not met, they will not be able to sit down and learn lessons at school or to play peacefully with their friends. Their brains will be distracted and stuck in the conflict, replaying the story over and over. We must pause what we're doing to address their emotions. Ways to do so include,

"Your love light looks dim, what happened?"

"I see your fists are clenched. Are you feeling angry?"

"Oh, yes, it's disappointing having to clean-up and end your activity."

At Chavitos, we will pause any lesson to address conflict and mend within our communities. We do this because we want our children to become boundary setters, clear communicators connected to the heart, thoughtful menders, and takers of responsibility for their choices and how they affect others. Especially at our preschool, we focus on taking the time to build this moral intelligence. We find this education is necessary and is the main work of this age group (and our middle school ages). These two groups are both in a special, sensitive period of their lives in which they are focused on emotions and learning to express them.

Centering Strategies for Conflict Resolution

Because we believe in normalizing conflict, we expect it to happen daily. If you are the director of a school or the head of a family, you know that we, as leaders, are faced with the result of conflict first. We can absorb some of it before it trickles down to our families and children. But this role of prime target and diffuser can be a tiring position. We are often the mediators of conflict between students, guides, neighbors, and government offices we work with to sustain and support our programs.

Within conflict, my goal is to slow down and intimately participate so people involved feel seen and heard. I find empathy is such a comforting balm to everyone involved. It soothes the wound and calms the burn sometimes present with conflict. The following is an example of moving through conflict at the school-wide level.

CASE STUDY

In hindsight, starting our preschool was easy breezy. We got permits, maxed our enrollment, and secured land with ease and grace. The preschool system seemed to fall into our laps like ripe fruit. Because it went so smoothly, I expected a similar process to happen when we started our K-8 program. Our K-8 program was originally located on a two-acre farm in a farm neighborhood with a new development bumping up to the land. We bought the land three weeks before school started. Things moved quickly and were full of gifts and ease, which my husband and I always interpret as a green light and go ahead from the universe.

But soon the picture-perfect situation of owning our own farm and hosting our program on it turned putrid. For the two years we were there, we had neighbors who harassed us by flipping-off parents, driving towards families' cars, and calling every organization they could to report us. Parents and guides felt increasingly unsafe. Fairly early in this conflict, I started the long process of filing an anti-harassment petition to get support. This was an extreme response, but the only other option was to not respond and continue to get harassed by the neighbor.

The conflict led to nine court dates! I had to miss class while other guides covered my students' lessons and I Zoomed-in to court from the shed. The final court date was the only one in which the neighbor attended. Because all our recorded and shared harassment wasn't done directly to me or my husband, our petition wasn't granted. The neighbor was severely warned but not held accountable for the fear he brought to our community.

But that wasn't the end of things. Throughout that time, and following that court date, we worked with the local permitting office to get permission to have our program on our farmland. This involved many unreturned phone calls to our case manager, in-person visits, and unreturned emails. It also led to over $25,000 in fees to the health department to install a converted well into a "Group B" well to serve the number of people at the program. Every week, it seemed, there was a new issue I would read about in an email, or through a certified letter in the mail. Either the code enforcer was being inundated by the neighbors and telling us to move our farmer's RV, we received a cease-and-desist letter from a lawyer for using the easement, or a government agency was checking to see if we had an after-school care program. The issues rolled in like a never-ending flood. Once one was handled, three more would pop up like the weeds covering our farm.

The hardest part of this situation was working with

antiquated systems. As a director, I often spent three hours of my administration morning hours on the phone or emailing someone to solve conflicts that were way out of my comfort zone or knowledge base. Then, I would drive to the farm, meditating on possible solutions. When I arrived, I would need to temporarily table all my concerns, my worries, and my fears that we would be shut down the next day or that the neighbor would come to our school and openly harm us.

I started to wonder if me carrying this weight alone was working or sustainable. Could I singlehandedly protect my community and parents? Did it resolve the problems quicker? Did it keep staff happy and unstressed at work so they could focus their attention on the students and teaching their intriguing lessons? What were my reasons for doing this alone?

I think a part of me was doing it all alone because I thought the conflict would end eventually. That resolution with the neighbor would happen. We would get the permit. The van we bought would reduce the traffic enough for the road to remain accessible to us. But, when none of that happened in our second year, I decided to try something new. I would find a way to share the burden I was holding with all this conflict.

I decided to be more honest about my burden and the amount of conflict I was facing as the director. I shared letters from the Department of Family and Children openly with staff. I let them know about the results of the court hearings I went to every other week for our anti-harassment petition. I let them see the tears of frustration I cried when we had to set the ninth court hearing date because the neighbor was not answering their door to be served. I also started to let the families of the children attending our program know about the progress we were making. I started sending a weekly update to a Learning Points document we regularly shared with families. Even if the update said, "no progress," or "nothing new to add," it was still open communication and a peek inside my worried heart. And the result was better than I expected. With this new information, parents asked how they could support me and the school. So, I shared permitting officer names, phone numbers, and locations for them to visit and call. Together, we put more pressure on our case manager to answer us, see us, and give us the information we needed.

This new method of transparency with conflict felt vulnerable and strange. But it aligned with our school's core values of authenticity and community. I had never personally experienced a leader using this strategy. It often felt like I was showing the soft underbelly of our organization and of myself to our wider community. I often wondered, would they think I was ditzy and unreliable? Would they judge my response to this crazy neighbor as not being sufficient? Would they think of my leadership as unconventional and ineffective? Would they still trust me with their children and enroll in our program? Would they stay with us through the unknowns and lack of answers?

Fast forward to today and I can say they did! We had four families who needed to pause for the remaining three months of the program year. But the other 17 families stayed with us and stepped up to our cries for help. The echo I most often heard from parents was, "We believe in you. You have solved a million other problems in the past. We believe you will continue to find solutions for us."

While parents said these things to encourage me, sometimes, the encouragement landed more as a burden. I asked myself, "Why is this different? What if I can't find solutions for these bigger problems? What if I am in over my head this time?"

Then, a cease-and-desist was declared to stop us from using the easement, which was the only way into our property. We then held a family meeting, created a poll, and eventually decided to move our K-8 program to a new location. This was not ideal with just three months of program left. Not ideal for my husband and my nervous system, either, which was already strung-out from the daily battles. We were almost broken by this decision. My husband wanted to call it quits. He had no more energy or heart in him after this level of defeat. In alignment with my new practice of transparency, I shared all this with the community. And you know what? They showed up! Instead of parents telling me, "*You* can do it! We believe in *you*." Their chants became, "*We* can do this. *We* believe in the power and importance of this community. *We* are stronger than this bullying neighbor. We are about *the people* that make up the community. It's not about *the place*." Somewhere along the way, the conflict had shifted to a collective effort and drive for resolution.

And we did find a solution. We partnered with an enrolled family to use their land for the K-8 program. The children packed up books, pencils, and the very simple basics, leaving every nonessential in place at the farm. Guides led us in a ritual of reflection, processing, and blessing our farmland as we transitioned off it. We walked around the farm sharing memories and tossing blessings of seeds as gratitude to her. We cried together and sang our favorite song, Pool of Love by Alexa Sunshine Rose. The van ride home was cricket-silent on that last day at the farm. Then, together as a community, we rebuilt. We helped construct a gazebo, rebuilt our geodome, hammered our composting toilet back together, made trips back and forth from the old farm to the new with our colored pencils, notebooks and pillows.

After everything was said and done, through 1-1 conversations and emails, I checked-in with parents about the process of moving the K-8 program from one location to another. I consistently heard feedback about how much they appreciated the level of transparency throughout the endeavor. They saw this conflict as one that was out of my control and hands. Like me, they felt this conflict was unfair, unjust, and similar to having a big bully pressure us until they got their way. These words were reassuring. They showed me that maybe this type of shared leadership, where conflict is laid out in the open instead of hidden away or shouldered by one person, could indeed work.

When I think back on this time of conflict, I think we were on to something big. Done are the ways of leadership that are top-down, with power in the hands of one person. We are now in the days of circular leadership, with more collaboration and opportunities for others to share their gifts and skills. My hats of director, visionary and guide are still respected, but now there's space for other perspectives and experiences that are essential to solving conflict we experience. Other people have an equal and rightful voice when finding solutions.

The truly amazing thing about modeling and being authentic around conflict is that our kids are watching. In the above conflict, the kids were involved in the heart of it. Their opinions were asked. They were included in our discussions. When we moved the school itself, they found important ways to contribute. All on their own, they decided to offer and make the adults tea. They set up an elaborate system in which different students took orders, made tea, delivered tea, and cleaned up. It was impressive! They had found their own ways to stay involved and help. This is why I don't hide conflict from children. They need to witness it. Witnessing conflict normalizes it. Conversely, when conflict is only behind closed doors, kids still see it, but hiding it away makes it scary and unpredictable to them. When it's experienced in front of them, or shared openly with them, they can observe and process it with others. The key to making this modeling effective is ensuring kids see the completion of the conflict. They need to see the resolution.

One of my favorite resources for handling conflict is called Turning Towards Each Other (2020), a model by Jovida Ross and Weyam Ghadbian. We've used it during our social justice lessons to help us learn about our own personal and dominant conflict archetype. I've also used it in staff meetings to help us learn about each other's response to conflict and how conflict tends to look for each of us. These conversations become touchstones which we can refer to. I use it at our home, as well, and I hope other parents do the same. Another curriculum we've been grateful to use is the Mosaic Project curriculum, called <u>Peacing it Together</u> (2003) by Brett Dennen. We use the songs and lessons in this curriculum to help children learn about big concepts like empathy, stereotypes, and conflict resolution. It also helps in using I-statements within catchy songs and engaging games and activities to support learning.

Like I mentioned earlier, conflict is a part of everyone's life. As I teach students about conflict resolution, I too slowly build up my skills. I pick a phrase here and store it in my toolbox or make a scribbled note in my mind of how a colleague responded to my direct conversation about an unsafe event that happened. Here are the steps I try to use in guiding resolution and the steps I try to use with my family and friends:

1. Pause and notice. Realize when I'm conflicted about something or someone. Say hi to it.
2. Get curious. Take space and time to figure out why things are happening as they are. Conflict shows me there is a boundary that's been crossed or a value that's been misunderstood or not shared.
3. Engage empathy by being curious. Ask yourself, where is the other person coming from? What needs do they have? What's happening in their life that would influence this decision? What about this isn't about me?
4. Gain perspective. If you need to get out of your head or get confirmation, ask for advice or perspective from others. Choose people who will be honest and objective with you. If you seek advice and perspective from a third party, try to share details without bias or opinion.

5. Self-examine. Be willing to change by remaining open. In every conflict, there are invitations for us to grow and change. This growth mindset leads to us improving and becoming better and more aware humans. Look for areas where you can change, ask for forgiveness, or learn.

6. Take ownership of your needs and wants. What do you need in the relationship and situation? What do you not want to continue? Think of how to make a clear statement of what you need. Give space and opportunity for others to share what they need or what they want to stop. If there are things in the situation that you can't control, then work on accepting those and letting go of your expectations.

7. Make a plan for mending and repairing. Put yourself in the other person's shoes. Think of what they might be feeling, or what they might need. Think of a solution that you can offer that would benefit both of you. Open your heart and listen to what other people need. Let them know if you can meet their requests. Sometimes, we need to have a conversation and compromise. Other times, we can't mend, and we need to adjust our relationship accordingly.

Invitations for Reflection

- What is your relationship to conflict? Do you love it, hate it, avoid it, or ignore it?

- Read *Turning Toward Each Other* and dive into the four archetypes of conflict. Which one do you naturally lean toward? What are your signs of being stuck or in flow?

- What resources do you use regarding conflict? How can you apply the lessons about conflict from those resources to your nature program policy?

Chapter 12
Maintain Your Wellness

Our mental health is directly connected to our wellness and that of our environment and community. If we are experiencing stress for sustained amounts of time, that stress will take a physical toll on us. We will likely start to see imbalances in our bodies that manifest like sickness. Most of the challenges I face in my directorship at Chavitos lead me to learning how to maintain personal and familial health and mental wellness. Daily, I am faced with decisions that require my family to honor our needs, to rest, to practice the pivot, and to adjust in the face of uncertainty. Let's look specifically at each of these practices below to give you a better understanding of how you might incorporate them into your family's path in life.

Honor Your Needs

It's essential to know yourself and anyone you're partnered with (in business, family, or friendships) well. Be honest with yourself and others about your limits, talents and capabilities. Taking myself as an example, I know that if my days are too packed with activities, I get stressed out. I need space to dream, ground and connect to the bigger source of inspiration or my wellness and happiness suffers. When this happens, all other aspects of my life are impacted. I find my temper is shorter with my children, I am less available for their needs, and I am grumpier about their requests. By the end of an overly busy day, I need to pass the baton to Jose and retreat to the space and quiet of my room. At that point, I am not available for the rest of the evening.

Jose is different. He has a wider and deeper capacity for interaction, banter, silliness and noise. His wellness looks like starting his morning chores with upbeat Latinx music pumping in his headphones. He then cooks breakfast and prepares for his day effortlessly and with high energy and joy. He greets his kids with a sweet and loud, "Buenos días!" once they're awake. Then, he hops on his bike and rides to the forest, all year around, even in pouring rain and freezing temperatures. After a day of work, he is still full of energy and ready to prepare dinner and tend to household chores, responsibilities, and personal projects. When he wakes up the next day, he's refreshed and ready to repeat his daily rituals.

Even though Jose and I are so different, we both value a connection to something bigger than ourselves. In my own life, that looks like maintaining a connection to astronomy and reading astrological reports each week. My favorite astrologer is Chani Nicoles, and their interpretations of the stars help me put the larger influences in my life into perspective. Studying astrology has shown me I'm not in control of the stars and their alignments, but I'm deeply impacted by them and live in a world that is also influenced by their squares, conjunctions and retrogrades. Jose likes to connect to the teachings of the Waldorf educational philosophy. These teachings help direct Jose as he moves through the world, reminding him of a perspective bigger than his own. I encourage you to find a source of connection to the world that is bigger than yourself, whether it's spiritual, philosophical, mathematical, or systemic. Doing so can remind you of your spark amidst the bigger universe we are all a part of.

Another personal need of mine is to connect with close friends on weekly walks, playdates, dinners and spa dates. Talking and connecting with these people brings my life into perspective and helps me eliminate distractions. I find I cherish feeling surrounded by those who truly see and celebrate me. When my friends' experiences of situations match or mirror mine, I feel more understood. When my friends show empathy for situations that might be like those they've experienced, I feel nurtured. I'm enriched by these friendships, as they fill my need for depth and authenticity in relationships.

Whether you are like me, Jose, or neither of us, it's important to know what sustains and supports your wellness. Ask yourself the following questions to get to know your needs.

- Do I feel nourished by noise or silence?
- What environments inspire me and make me feel alive?
- What makes me tired?
- When tired, how do I like to recharge?
- What parts of my day do I complain about the most? What is something I can do to change that?
- What's my favorite part of the day? How do I bring the elements that make it special into other parts of my day?
- What types of people do I not enjoy being around? How can I create more distance or reduce my time around them?
- What types of people do I enjoy being around? How can I increase my time with them?

If you feel out of balance, remember you have the power to make changes to your lifestyle and days. Reflecting on your answers to the above questions will help guide you to an increased awareness, and ultimately, wellness, in the midst of our modern world.

Rest

The biggest gift I have given myself in my life as an entrepreneur and mother is permission to slow down. It's important to give ourselves permission to rest. We need to notice when we are hustling at full speed and then to also put on the brakes. In *Living Resistance: An Indigenous Vision for Seeking Wholeness Every Day* (2023), Kaitlin B. Curtice shares her experience, "... rest is not earned but belongs to us, to our bodies, simply because we are human." The human way isn't to always rush and multitask. It should include moments of rest and relaxation, as well. Some of the practices I follow to find daily rest are:

- Complete chores and activities in silence.
- Walk without distraction to notice what's happening around me.
- Do one task at a time.
- Say no to a lot of activities. Only say yes to that which brings us joy and aligns with our values.
- Enjoy "home days" where you stay home and rest, play, read, or putter around the home.
- Create a daily schedule that includes space for dreaming, tending and detailing. Consider these pockets of time as sacred. They will help you do your best work from a well-rested state.

Handling Uncertainty

When building anything new, you will be faced with a lot of unknowns and surprises. And, when we are presented with change, we have opportunities to reflect and then respond. When building our K-8 program, we experienced a lot of uncertainty. Remember the story I told about facing conflict with our neighbor at the K-8 program? At that time, we spent an entire year not knowing if we would be approved for a permit or supported with an anti-harassment petition. Every day, we faced a new and previously unknown challenge. This was a really hard time for me. But I knew then, as I know now, that managing my wellness includes managing my response to uncertainty. I must not let uncertainty drag me into preoccupation and anxiety. One of the ways I do this is by utilizing a helpful resource on the growth mindset, as Carol Dweck has taught us. Dweck's work focuses on developing a growth mindset rather than a fixed one. Here are two strategies I use to respond to uncertainty:

- **Learn the power of "yet."** Yet acknowledges the learning curve we all are on. Remember, our abilities can grow through our hard work. We might not have the knowledge of how to handle a current uncertainty *yet*. Tell yourself, "I don't know how to do _____ yet. I'm going to ask some experts for support and advice."

- **Praise yourself for the things you are doing well in a situation**. Honor your process and progress in figuring something out instead of focusing or getting stuck on achieving an end goal.

Another thing that helps me face uncertainty is listing the things I can control in a situation. I know I can't control whether a guide moves to the East Coast or if a neighbor is intimidating us. But I *can* control using

my resources and skills to hire a new guide or trying to learn the ins and
outs of a legal system. I can't control the forest fires and smoke levels caused
by our climate crisis. But I *can* use my resources to create a smoke and fire
protocol to keep students and guides safe. I can't control the number of
weeds that flood our farm site, but I *can* learn and educate myself about
permaculture techniques. Knowing what I can and can't control helps me
focus my energy on the right direction, leading me to pivot with changes
instead of floundering and sinking under uncertainty. It's also helpful to
reflect on past experiences that were also challenging, of which, we made it
through victoriously. Self-talk, like "I know our community is supportive
because we've moved locations before and they supported us with the
move," can help you get unstuck from the fear of uncertainty and moving
toward solutions.

Practicing the Pivot

A few years ago, I remember hearing the word "pivot" used in a
conversation that changed how I thought about the word's meaning. I'd
gone to a community dinner, and I had complained about how three people
had ghosted me in one week at work. That week had been an important
time in my life, and I wanted to garner empathy about the difficulty of the
situation from those I loved, especially as it related to being an educational
director. After the dinner, a friend texted me, saying, "it must be hard to
pivot so often." That word, *pivot*, stuck with me. I liked it. It offered such
an accurate description of what was required of me during that week. In the
face of adversity or unforeseen circumstances, I had chosen to move forward
and carry out unexpected work. That is pivoting.

Being a director of an alternative educational program has given me
plenty of practice at pivoting. When 17 beautiful faces look at me, ready

for a social justice lesson, but it's five minutes past the starting time and our guest teacher still hasn't arrived, I pivot. I pull a lesson from my head and draw the children's attention to me. The lesson goes well. Do I like coming up with and implementing a lesson on the spot? No. Does it add to my stress level? Immensely. But was it necessary? Absolutely. Sometimes we must do what life asks of us, whether or not we are "good at it" or want to carry it out.

Some people are naturally good at pivoting. They are gifted with this skill. They can heartily laugh, nonchalantly shrug, and easefully adjust to change. Jose can do all of those things with ease. I believe his ability to pivot contributes to his skill as a guide. Unsurprisingly, he is one of my greatest teachers in life. He is always able to adjust to whatever is in front of him and find a viable path forward. Admittedly, he is also one who I show the most resistance to. When I'm crying, burning red, or wanting to stomp my feet in a tantrum, he isn't fazed. He somehow maintains his cool.

I suspect his upbringing in Guatemala provided ample opportunities for him to practice pivoting in life. In Guatemala, plans rarely go according to schedule. A short hour of traveling can turn into a full day of hot, sticky, inching, and grudging traffic with no notice. It often feels hard to plan, hard to prevent, and hard to predict sudden change when my family and I are living in Guatemala. Yet, that is exactly why I like being there. Guatemalan culture includes space for the blessed result of conflict and sideway plans, whatever it may be. Through this aspect of life in Guatemala, I have learned not to hide from conflict or hardship, as those very things encourage us to embrace pivoting.

Continuously working on my ability to pivot, and my relationship to change, has helped me both personally, at home, and professionally, as a director. Pivoting helps me let go of perfectionism and move into a flow state. I have learned to hold some things loosely. Hopefully, this psychological muscle-building will allow for more grace, ease, and laughter around challenges we and our children encounter in the future.

We should ask ourselves, what opportunities are in front of us right now that invite us to pivot? Of course, living in rural Guatemala among puttering tuk-tuks and zipping chicken buses is not an opportunity everyone has. But there are dozens of opportunities presented to us each day. We might find an opportunity to pivot when we realize we have no eggs or coffee for our breakfast meal. Or maybe we get stuck on the edge of a protest that closes the highway for four hours on our way to work. If the opportunity to pivot shows up in our cards today, hopefully we'll be able to laugh, find a path forward by moving in a new direction, and tuck away a bit of knowledge for another day when we need to take a deep breath and try it again. I wish us all luck and the ability to pivot with ease and grace.

Invitations for Reflection

- Consider your responses to the questions presented earlier in this chapter. What are two or three action steps you will take toward bolstering your own wellness?

- Think about a few instances in your workplace when you had to pivot. How did you do? What are some ways you could have improved or pivoted more smoothly?

- Think about times when students in your life have modeled pivoting. How has their ability to pivot inspired you?

Chapter 13

Define Your Leadership

Who are the world's best and most effective leaders? Who comes to mind? I think of Bill Strickland, Chani Nicholas, and Dolly Parton. Now, who are the worst leaders you can think of, both past and present? What distinguishes one group from the other? What traits make the best leaders? Personally, I believe bravery, activism, justice, authenticity, connection to people, integration to a cause, sacrifice, and inspirational speakers with new ideas are traits that great leaders move through the world with. These are the characteristics I want to bring into my own leadership.

Leadership can be a lonely place to inhabit. Being a leader naturally puts you on a mountain top, and people are often drawn to your ways, values and causes. They follow you because they see something they want to spark or ignite in themselves. This gathering and uniting of vision is how strong and influential communities are created.

If you hope to open an alternative, outdoor education program of your own one day, or even simply participate in one, you must find and build with people who share your values. This facilitates alignment across multiple layers, including social interactions, educational programming, group dynamics, troubleshooting, and solution-building. Creating a program with people who share values with you creates ease and strength. In your leadership, trust that the connections you need for your collective will come. Cast a wide net of vision and see what manifests in your life. Connect with people who are walking their path and live their calling and see how doing so can intertwine with your calling to braid a strong, multi-strand cord.

As a leader, it's crucial that we also consider our relationship to power and decision-making. Take a close look at how you want to lead, even if you do not plan to hold a leadership position. Leadership is a way of being, not a role one fills. And in small communities like ours (homeschooling co-ops), there will inevitably come a time when you are asked to lead in some way, shape or form.

Earlier in this book, I shared with you how I've started approaching leadership differently. My goal is that at Chavitos, "leader" is a shared title. I, the director, cannot carry it alone. Nor do I want to, especially if I am in unknown territory, which I often am. I don't think one person can be an expert on everything and meet the needs of everyone in the community. As with everything else in life, we need to diversify. There are times when I need to make snap decisions, and I can't take as much time as I would like to strategize. This is when I need to call on other expert voices. To be able to do that, though, I had to embark on a long, multi-year journey of changing my leadership style that started with releasing control, as you'll read about in the following pages:

CASE STUDY

For many years, I looked at what the next step might be in learning to share my responsibilities as a leader. First, I stepped out of teaching preschool and trusted that Jose was ready for the challenge of leading the preschool without me. At the time, we knew creating success for Jose as a leader meant finding co-guides who would balance his gifts and gaps. Next, I hired guides to teach subjects I didn't want to and an administrator who is talented with details and communication. Then, I took the most exciting step just a few months ago: hiring co-directors for our leadership team.

Organizationally, we now have two co-directors on a leadership team with me to help expand our program with their personalized gifts and talents. When I put the team together, I tried to call in people with different assets, that way we could delegate tasks to each other based on our skill sets and capacity. This strategy encouraged me to notice other people's gifts, lean on those gifts as I delegate accordingly, and then rest knowing someone capable is taking on necessary work. I can express my vision to our leadership team and then trust someone to execute it using their gifts. This allows me, and us, to move with ease and hold each other accountable.

I had to wait for a beat until the perfect two people came into my life to form this leadership team, but it was worth the wait. Now, we can expand to create a separate middle school modeled after Montessori philosophy. We can offer field trips, more guest speakers, seasonal celebrations, and student-led conferences. We can also offer special education support. This sharing of leadership has brought Chavitos to a new level. It also saved my sanity at the same time!

This leadership strategy requires me to hold strong boundaries around what is and is not my work to take on as a leader. It also requires that I remain open enough to look around at people in my community and try to understand, on a fundamental level, what their gifts are. This allows me to pull from a wider pool of information when I am troubleshooting issues in our programs, and ultimately, be comfortable and informed enough to ask people to use their gifts for the benefit of the community when the time comes.

This strategy has taken a long time to develop. It takes time to get to know people and the layers of lived experience they bring to their work. But the more informed and honest I am about what I need, the more I can trust the soundness of the solutions we come up with as a team and as a wider community.

It is also important that I let go of my expectations of how things will work out. In part, this is because I move fast and pay attention to timing. So, when the time comes for decisions to be made or action to be carried out, I need timing to be tight and communication to be on-point. Then, after I've done everything, I can, I try to let go of control and trust that what needs to happen will. I must trust the process.

Don't get me wrong, doing things this way is not my preference. I am a perfectionist. I'm detailed. I prefer to solve problems by myself and often move faster than people around me. I also hold my plans loose. I try to trust that the best thing will happen for everyone involved. I trust spirit. I wouldn't be able to do my work otherwise. This new leadership strategy, though, requires that I slow myself down. Yet, it also allows me to trust my intuition. Sometimes, I wake up at two o'clock in the morning with a fully formed plan. I know that in those instances, spirit gives me everything I need to solve my challenges. Figuring out how to set up evacuation routes for each of our programs came to me in one of these instances. One night, I woke up and I knew exactly what needed to be done. Later that morning, I talked to staff, and we were able to build and implement our evacuation routes within the same day.

In the past, I used to try to muscle and power my way through my toughest leadership challenges. Over time, and by using the power of self-reflection, I noticed in myself a comfort with paternalism and the idea that authority figures "know best." In paternalistic leadership, authority figures decide on behalf of others, and this is usually accompanied by a sense of urgency attached to decision making. *There's never enough time*, paternalism tells us. This was modeled, taught and expected from me by the dominant culture leadership I saw in my churches, classrooms and sport teams. But this leadership style has always felt limiting. It perpetuates cycles of domination and control. So, I started to focus on leadership that feels different. I asked myself, "Who around me is doing leadership differently?" Chris Vega of Blue Cactus Press is one example. They start book meetings with the open-ended question, "What's going on?"

This often leads our meetings off topic, but into beautiful creative spaces where collaboration blooms. I feel seen and celebrated and my needs are met. In *Turning Towards Each Other: A Conflict Workbook,* authors Jovida Ross and Weyam Ghadbian say,

"There are also hundreds of years of non-dominant cultural practices of caring, interdependence, and resilience that we can each draw on to cultivate a life-giving culture. When we are proactive about reflecting on these dynamics, and talking about them regularly, we become more aware of when our behaviors are shaped by dominant culture. When we are more aware we can choose regenerative practices instead."

I have also learned that it is much more efficient, and better for everyone involved, if I use my brain and heart first, then my voice. It's easier to stand in community when I am unsure of how to move forward and allow a more natural melding together of information, resources, and people instead of pushing through the situation with my organizational power. Doing so has proven to be a more powerful leadership stance than standing alone, wielding my power, and moving quickly.

Nowadays, as the founder and co-director of Chavitos, I use a structure of mutuality to support our organization. I utilize it in three main areas: with guides, students, and parents. I have found that as a leader, I must not only keep my team of guides in the loop about what I am thinking about and the decisions that need to be made, but I must also be completely honest with them. This way, I don't have to relay a ton of information to them at once and I can maintain a high degree of transparency throughout the process. I offer little bits of information to my team as they come to me. This helps me pull people in and keep them close.

Parents are another important part of effective, mutual leadership teams in educational programs. Our K-8 program is structured as a co-op because the families are homeschooling their children and we are partnering with them to further educate our collective children. This means we must adopt leadership mindsets that are effective for this particular type of partnership. As a community, we are intentionally trying to move away from dominant cultural practices and toward dismantling white supremacy culture. We use the following content, found within Turning Toward Each Other by Jovida Ross & Weyam Ghadbian (2020), to guide us in this collective work.

> "We live in a world shaped by hundreds of years of collective, structural harms (the legacies of brutal colonization, slavery, patriarchy) that shape the culture we live in. That means these patterns have shaped us too, and we must assume they are present in our relationships. To release the patterns of domination and violence, it's helpful to acknowledge how we may have internalized them and are unconsciously acting them out. (p.1)."

Parents and Guides need to be fully submerged in practices that dismantle white supremacy culture so they can model, teach and support students in the enactment of them. Our hope is that if we can use this with our guides and parents, they will hopefully use it with children in their care and structure their classes and teachings around these beliefs and practices of mutuality. Here are some leadership tenets related to mutuality that I have noticed exist in our educational systems after years of this constant practice:

- We acknowledge Power (in all its manifestations). Acknowledging power differentials and how they impact individual and group experiences is critical to our success. We ask, *who doesn't have power right now? Who does? How is that working for everyone involved? How can we balance this so those with a lot of power can share their power with those who don't have much?* Balancing power might look like an older student asking younger students for their opinions. Or the loudest students in a group asking and listening to quieter students. Those with strong opinions could take time to hear those who normally don't voice opinions.

- We support individual freedom and autonomy within our group's purpose. Things don't have to be mandatory. If a child's body has a different need (like to engage in movement during a sit-down lesson), they can go and find ways to meet their needs. If a child needs more rest, they can spend movement time taking care of that need. We accept and support each other when our autonomy calls for accommodating different needs.

- We sit with our own discomfort with differing opinions, especially if we have more positional, social or economic power. It's okay to not agree with each other. Instead of bullying or powering our way through a situation to gain compliance, though, we can just acknowledge how a situation challenges us. We can say, *Ok, your decision to do____ really challenges me… I would like to know more about your point of view. Why do you feel that way?* We teach children to be curious around other people's opinions or decisions so they can remain soft, teachable, and open. This takes practice and that's why we start teaching it when children are young.

- We actively invite feedback. It is very important for those in power to hold space for receiving feedback. We should invite feedback regularly. Feedback is strongest when an experience is fresh. The more we practice receiving feedback in low-stakes situations, the more comfortable we'll get with it. Then, it'll be easier to receive feedback in higher-stakes situations.

- Feedback should be descriptive.

- We use language like, *I saw, I heard, I noticed...*

- We use verbs to describe the action we observed and are offering feedback on.

- We ground our observations with specific information instead of broad generalizations.

- We use feedback to share appreciation. Feedback about what works is incredibly useful, especially when we let each other know why or how something worked well for us.

- Feedback should be constructive.

- We teach and model language like, *I wish... What if...*

- We embrace tension in groups and consider moments of tension as opportunities for reflection, surfacing new insights, and rebalancing. We learn through mistakes and keep a growth mindset when addressing our blunders or any hurt we've caused.

Learning is not done just within the boundaries of our learning environments. We trust and expect these beliefs to support our children in other settings, like at home. We trust that the effects will trickle down and impact our whole community. Parents will see their children using these strategies of mutuality, even if that means parents may be called out by youth, or vice versa, when acting against principles of mutuality. This process will become the norm for our children's generation as they take on leadership positions.

As our children grow and take on varying roles and responsibilities, it's important to practice decision-making. In some cases, **self-stewardship** is the appropriate tactic to teach. Self-stewardship is where operational decisions that don't impact others substantively are left to an individual to make, rather than whomever is "in charge" or in a position of power over them.

There are also situations where it is best to make decisions as a **consensus**. This applies to decisions that require full buy-in for successful implementation. An example would be a moment when we need to figure out what our guides' weekly rhythms are going to look like. Sometimes we call a meeting with all our guides, or other times, we might open-up a conversation for feedback and questions to gain guidance on how to finalize plans. Another example would be if I propose to the families at our co-op the idea of expanding our winter break from two to four weeks. I would wait to hear if there were any objections, and then if so, we would address them as a group.

A third method of decision-making in community is **consultative**. This occurs when we need to make decisions that will impact others significantly and need a single point of accountability. An example would be if we started a middle school and wanted to decide how it should be structured. We would base our decision on guides' observations, parents' needs, and what students want or are ready for.

Lastly, there is a decision-making method that is based on a **leader's singular choice**. This occurs when we need to make decisions that have clearly defined choices to pick from, and that impact many individuals, and for which consensus is impractical or not necessary. An example would be when we are trying to decide if our program should stay on our farmland, move to a new space at the end of the year, or move to a new space right now.

Being a great leader means discerning which decision-making method is best for any given situation. This leadership model roots my perspective in a leader's values and the values of the people around them. When we live out our values in leadership positions, the impact of our decisions trickles into other aspects of our lives. This is why leaders need to be balanced. As leaders, we should aim to use our brain and lead with our heart. And we should aim for connection and intimacy.

Intimacy needs to be modeled. When intimacy is modeled, it becomes expected. Then it can be more fully received. When people give us doors and openings into their lives, usually through small talk, it gives a leader the chance to get to know them more deeply. One question alone, in a casual conversation, can open people up for beautiful connection points. It also fosters an atmosphere of gratitude and acceptance, which goes a long way. I try to model it in staff meetings, emails, and in person-to-person interactions.

Leaders should be approachable yet have boundaries. Sometimes, the boundaries I hold (or which anyone holds) can scare people off. Sometimes, people are hesitant to share their own boundaries. They may be afraid to "add to a leader's plate." But this approach puts leaders on a pedestal and removes them, even if by one or two steps, from a level of intimacy that is necessary to lead well. To combat this, a leader can be open about their weaknesses and struggles. This re-positions them back at the same level with their support system, team, or community. Great foundations are built around leadership that is mutual and where power is shared. Hopefully, in the future, we will have more organizations and leaders to point to when asked, "Who is your most influential leader?" Maybe one day, some of our current children will be on your list and known worldwide as influencers of change.

Invitations for Reflection

- Who do you consider to be the most inspirational leader? What traits do they possess that you want to cultivate?

- What type of leadership feels most comfortable to you? Does that leadership style feel sustainable to you? Does it feel equitable? Why or why not? Who benefits most from that leadership style?

- Consider the decision-making methods listed earlier in the chapter. Which method is one you want to try? Who will you try it with?

Epilogue

We often think resistance requires being on the front line, protesting, marching or attending special events. But living resistance is a lifestyle. It includes having a lazy Sunday, baking, relaxing, and finding peace. It also includes living out resistance to our nation's dominant culture, which values production over rest. The ways we live out our resistance can be simple, but often, they are complex, pushing us to bridge the gap between our philosophical ideals and daily actions. When these two things align, we are culture-building, future-visioning, and world-building. It is from this place that we should teach our children how to live. We must teach them to notice, build, and rest from this place, rather than a place of misalignment.

This dedication to living in alignment with our personal values, despite the misunderstanding we face from mainstream society, is what makes living resistance a spiritual act. How could it not be? Living in alignment with our values allows us to step into the most actualized versions of ourselves, to live up to our highest potential. The following story is about my own path of resistance and how it led me to founding Chavitos. I share it with the intention to inspire and motivate you to find your own forms of resistance in response. May you see how my calling was obvious from a young age. I believe you too have a clear path of personal resistance. It's not too complicated or hidden if you reflect on what brings you light and energy.

* * * *

I grew up connected to the earth. I've always had a heart for nature. As a baby, my parents dipped me in the cooling waters of Barton Springs in Austin, Texas, where I was born. As I grew, I continued to love playing outdoors. My dad took me fishing and let me run outside in mud, shirtless and in my boots for long periods of time. I was outside all day, doing what other kids raised in the 80's did: building forts out of building scraps, wading in muddy creeks, and cruising around the neighborhood on banana seat bikes. I kept so busy my parents didn't know where I was. As a young elementary student, I surfed with my father in the warm waters of San Diego. He taught me how to duck under waves, holding my breath until we popped back up to the surface, and how to paddle to get positioned just perfectly under the wave. It felt safe under his guidance on the shared board, but also scary. Huge ocean waves dominated my nightmares for years as I processed how small and vulnerable I felt. My dad taught me to respect the ocean, and I learned water brought me a deep sense of calm. When we moved to Oregon at the age of nine, I spent time making traps and forts with the neighbor kids. I learned to play in the rain and the magic of puddles. We were left to create, to find solutions, to get dirty. I felt all children should have a similar childhood.

Even though we moved around a lot before our final move to Oregon, at twelve- years-old, I still lived in this same Hercon Circle neighborhood. That was where I started babysitting and realized I enjoyed and had skills for working with young children. My love for nature grew alongside my love for children. After a trip to Kaliningrad, Russia, during my senior year in high school, I was especially aware of those vulnerable in the orphanage systems of other countries. It was life changing to see how other people lived, how educational systems functioned abroad, and how orphanages were run. The children I met in Russia were so hungry for love and attention that I could feel their longing every time I stepped into a room with them. They all wanted to show me their space, and the few precious belongings hidden under their pillows.

Throughout my life, and as far back as I can remember, I have felt a lack of belonging within various organizations and social structures I participated in. Even though I was loved and my physical needs were met by my family, I always felt different and alone. It seemed like everyone at birth received a user manual for the human experience. I had one too, but when I followed it, I was met with blank stares, confusion and irritated redirection. What mattered to me didn't seem to matter to others. My impact on others was often negative or exhausting. This made it easier for me to see others who were holding the same questions I was: "Am I loved?... Am I ok?... If I show up fully, will you still care for me?"

These inquiries were also tied to my strong sense of justice and humanitarian work. I lived by the rule of Mother Teresa: live a simple life so others can simply live. In elementary school, I read biographies of historical figures who fought injustice by acts of mercy and kindness. Hungry people were fed. Enslaved people were led to freedom. Miles were marched for equality. I soaked up stories of struggles and victories. I decided I wanted to dedicate my life to doing the same. I was inspired to advocate and love those the world deemed "unlovable."

A common theme of my life has been noticing and questioning my lack of belonging. *Why did I feel like I didn't belong?* I always wondered why I didn't fit in. *Should I change to be accepted? Did others experience this sensation, too? Was my biracial identity a factor?*

If you remember or lived through it, the 80's were a "color blind" era, and one that also lacked accessible neuroscience tools for everyday people. A lot of parents weren't emotionally connected to children, and I don't remember talking very openly about racial identity with adults around me when I was a small child. Even though my mother is Chinese and my father is Scottish and Irish, I only knew something was different about me because everyone I met was curious about my racial identity. I was approached constantly and asked, "What are you?"

I never saw examples of families like mine on the shows I watched, in the books I read, or in the community I lived in. At that time, Beaverton, Oregon, was predominantly white. Consequently, I had no words to define this experience of having brown skin because no one around me was having nuanced conversations about racial identity. It was only ever, "Where are you from?"

Don't get me wrong, the fact that we were a biracial family wasn't ignored intentionally, and my mom wasn't ashamed of her Chinese ancestry. But society had taught her that her ancestors were culturally unimportant. She was taught this not by her parents, but by the Oklahoma community where she was raised. In both my mother and grandmother's time, assimilation canceled and trumped any pride in cultural identity that survived the immigration process. This is how, within my family, our cultural and ethnic Chinese roots were nearly erased in a single generation. Assimilation made cultural ghosts out of us, as it does most people. It stripped us of our cultural identity. I too was shrouded in this disillusion. When I was young, I overheard someone say that I was nice because all Chinese people are nice. This comment impacted me, like a hidden wound that didn't appear until my 30's. It felt like internal bleeding, and it was making me sick.

I remember once when I was a young adult, I was looking through my mom's high school yearbook and noted that she and her two brothers were the only people of color in the entire school. When I asked her about this, she replied, "…at least we weren't Black." That kind of response is an automatic and racist response for many people within the Asian community. As troubling as this comment is, it has been a key that's helped me identify what racism looks like for Asians. Asian culture has been responded to with dismissal of more indirect racism in mainstream U.S. culture. We also face daily stereotyping and microaggressions. This diverts the conversations surrounding racism and racial equity away from those who perpetuate it and instead keep the victims of it pinned against each other. Which, in my opinion, is the best strategy for serving the colonizer's energy and agenda.

The racism I experienced growing up was often so subtle I easily missed it. This created confusion about who I was and where I found (or didn't find) belonging. Even when I'd earned a scholarship from a Chinese culture organization and attended a celebratory dinner surrounded by other Chinese people, I struggled with imposter syndrome. *Was I really Chinese? Did I really deserve this scholarship reserved for Chinese people? Do many biracial people struggle to fit into an ill-fitting identity?* I think so, and I think that's where we get racial labels such as "Oreos" (someone who is Black and white) or "Bananas" (an Asian American person acting too white).

Now, looking back, I can see this "othering" happened in hundreds of instances before I ever applied for the scholarship I mentioned previously. Every time I had to fill out a form, I was asked what my race was, but I was only allowed to check one box, white or Asian. While pumping gas, I was constantly asked, "Where are you from?" by strangers who were excited to see someone who looked like them. In every group I was a part of, I would count how many other people of color were there with me. Usually, I was the only one. I was also different from all the people I saw on TV. Biracial people were not represented on television at the time. I looked different from any people in power, and even different from people in my family.

My misfit mindset went beyond my racial identity. It was also related to my interests and mindset. I looked and acted differently than my family members. In my youth, I didn't care about the American dream or which movie star had the latest haircut. I wanted to talk about things that I felt *really mattered*. I had no tolerance for small talk. My heart was set on connecting deeply and meaningfully with people, instead.

Comments from my family added to my ongoing confusion. My mom would tell me I "wasn't very Chinese." *What does that even mean?*, I asked myself each time. *What traits am I missing? Can I cultivate those traits so I can connect more with her?* When I asked my mother these questions, she said being Chinese meant to be loyal, quiet, and reserved. *Yep,* I thought, *I will never be those things and don't plan to be.* My aunt would always remind me, "Remember you are also half Celtic." Fearing her heritage would be erased from my personal testimony. No doubt a lack of belonging was my biggest wound. But I believe we all have big wounds. Those wounds can be full of pain, confusion or rejection, like mine, but they can also be the perfect soil for a seed of healing and medicine to grow from.

I believe my thirst for belonging was one of the reasons I connected with nature to the degree I did as a child. Nature was a place where I felt deeply welcomed just as I was. It could hold my loud, spicy energy and my strong opinions. It was a place of deep importance and conversations I had there with plants and animals mattered. Each part of the ecosystem was essential, just like I was essential to the world. Nature was magical and unpredictable. Gaia could be fierce and burn down a forest with her fire. Or she could be gentle like a breeze cooling us down on a hot day. She could invite me toward water to dunk in or set a strong boundary of protection with a wasp nest or thicket of brambles. She was so complicated, yet so simple at the same time. I liked that depth. She was strong and could fix problems others created. She was wise and created solutions. There was purpose and intricate intention in everything she created. She was an artist that created awe inspiring details and broad strokes of the sunset or towering mountain peaks. I could see my complicated self in her. Because I adored her so deeply, she became a key ingredient to the medicine I was creating. That medicine had a base of not belonging that was ground up into something different via the nourishment of nature. My healing balm and life's work was transforming as I grew.

As I readied myself to begin college, I faced the ever-iconic question of *what am I going to major in*? After a few bumps in the road, I settled on a degree in education. At the time, I didn't envision myself becoming a teacher, but education made sense because it would allow me to spend time with children. My heart was inspired by humanity and social justice. I wanted to work with children who had been marginalized, like children who had been orphaned, and provide them with love and acceptance. *Where did the most vulnerable children live?* I asked myself. Wherever that was, I wanted to go there.

After finishing my degree in Education from Pacific Lutheran University in December 2000, I felt ready to start my journey of helping those in vulnerable communities. So, I went to Mozambique and learned and taught under Heidi Baker. Baker describes her role as working with the "poorest of the poor" and had a reputation of doing service like that of Mother Theresa. I aligned with her vision and humanitarian heart, and I spent two months at a school learning and practicing how to live out the mantra, "there is always enough," with her.

After that, I lined up work with a non-profit called Empowering Lives International (ELI) in which I would live in Kenya and support their child sponsorship program. At ELI, we connected sponsors with children living in Children's Homes. However, before I could make my way there, I got malaria while backpacking through Tanzania and Kenya. This sickness, and a new budding romantic relationship with an Australian man I met while in Mozambique, made me question my next step of working with children in Kenya. I followed my heart and that man to Byron Bay, Australia, where I learned how to drum and cook big pots of soup for the homeless community. When that budding relationship wilted, I reconnected with my vision of serving children in need, but first I needed to return home to heal my broken heart.

Once I was back home in Tacoma, I was hired to teach fifth grade at an inner-city school while living with friends. This job was difficult, as I was used to working with younger students who would join me in singing as we transitioned to the carpet to read aloud. Older students, even at just eleven years old, had heavy backpacks filled with trauma and heartbreak. I didn't know how to work through that with children of that age group. I put in a year of hard work and had several victories with amazing students. However, my heart was still set on the journey I had abandoned in Africa.

I decided to apply for an international teaching position in Lagos, Nigeria. I was hired, and I lived there for two chaotic years. That experience was one for a separate book altogether. I will say, though, that during that time, I learned that fast and crowded city life wasn't my jam. I tried to spend as much time at the beach and nature preserves as I could, but it was difficult to travel due to local traffic, which people call, "Go Slows," in pigeon. When not stuck in traffic trying to escape the city on new adventures, I studied for my National Boards Certification, a voluntary and elite certification that identifies teachers who meet very specific standards through a performance-based, peer-reviewed series of assessment components. Once I held my National Boards Certification, and with a reputation as an excellent teacher, I had more choices regarding where I would go after my two years in Nigeria ended. My options included an invitation to teach in England from a past family who attended AISL my first year of teaching; teaching at The Green School in Bali, which was a wild concept of outdoor and holistic education; or returning to Tacoma and getting support from the local school district to get Montessori trained and then teach at a public Montessori school. I decided on the third option and packed my shipping container for a return home. I would be a Montessori public school teacher in Tacoma, Washington.

In Tacoma, I met a friend, Connie, while going through my Montessori training. Connie had just returned from teaching at an international school in Thailand. We became quick friends, and the following summer, Connie invited me to join a group going to Guatemala to serve with a non-profit called Camino Seguro, or Safe Passage. Camino Seguro was started with one woman's humble vision to touch the lives of the poorest, most at-risk children in Guatemala City. It has grown significantly since its early days in 1999. The team of women I went with ranged in age from 18 to 66 years old. We were all meant to serve as clowns (yes, actual clowns) and would connect with students in the organization's Ludi Club, which offered clown performances and taught circus skills. It was there, in Guatemala City, as I volunteered for a short two weeks, that I met my future husband and co-founder of Chavitos, Jose.

Jose and I met while he was helping put stilts on children who would perform for our group. This group of children was used to performing around their neighborhood. On one of our last nights in Guatemala City, a few people from my group and I invited Jose and his co-worker, Estuardo, to visit us in Antigua for a night of salsa dancing. I remember not being too excited to dance because we had already done so the night before. But I told my friends, "If Jose is there, then I'll stay." I had no idea that this decision would impact my life so deeply. That night, I watched Jose walk across the central plaza. We linked arms and started a conversation that eleven years later, hasn't stopped.

Later that year, after I finished my volunteer work, I returned to Guatemala during my two-week Christmas break to spend more time with Jose. Jose lived about an hour away from where we met. I had such a wonderful time and fell in love on that trip. I returned to Guatemala again during my two weeks of spring break. And again, that summer.

When I wasn't on vacation visiting Jose in Guatemala, I continued to teach at Geiger Montessori in Tacoma. I ended up teaching there for six years in the lower elementary school. During that time, I fell in love with alternative education and the philosophy of Montessori. I improved and refined my teaching skills and learned more about myself as a learner through the hands-on curriculum of Montessori. During one of the yearly conferences, I learned about the work of Brene Brown, Jon Young, and Richard Louve, the author of *Last Child in the Woods*. These three guides helped me to define my values and educational beliefs. The power of authenticity, using nature as a teacher, and the social urgency of getting kids involved in nature all became part of my foundational education practice. I noticed that the skills Louve championed are naturally taught in and through nature. All the while, my belief in the public system disintegrated. I and a lot of other teachers were becoming disillusioned with the demands of standardized teaching, the sterilization of our approach, and the limitations of personal impact.

In the eleven years of teaching I had under my belt at the time, I became deeply connected with many students who struggled to be supported by the education system. One of my favorite students was named

Jared. Jared was so strange! He had a lilting voice, he talked with active hands, and his mom would come to school with a parrot on her shoulder and bird poop splattered down her back. The two of them were quite a pair. I loved Jared, and I could see his inner treasure. He was creative and expressive and struggled to sit still during lessons and to keep up with the pace of whole group lessons or academic expectations. Every day, I would work to change the labels that people placed on Jared and the reputation he held with other students. His misfit reputation was born from a narrative repeated by children, but also by other staff. I advocated and tried to rewrite his narrative. He was often referred to as weird, explosive, and unstable, but I wanted to shift the narrative to unique, passionate, and creative. Everyone, including Jared and other children who don't immediately fit in with their peers, deserves to belong in their communities. As a person with power in a classroom, I knew I could cultivate some of that with Jared and his classmates. We each have the power to do this, to see who isn't fitting in because of negative stereotypes and narratives and weave gold into their stories. As parents, guides, and community members, it is up to us to help children see themselves as the treasure they are. This became my justice mission with Jared and all the students whose needs weren't met in the system.

As with each of my different teaching experiences — traditional public schools, private international schools, and a public Montessori school — my time teaching helped me improve my skills and discover my own personal teaching philosophy. I found that I loved the diversity of my classrooms in Tacoma; I loved the world experience students in Nigeria brought to the classroom; I loved the hands-on learning materials and honoring of children I found in Montessori philosophy.

But there was also so much I didn't enjoy in the educational systems I'd taught in. I noticed play was essentially erased from the kindergarten classrooms during the decade in which I'd been teaching. The playdough, class pets, and kitchen sets were replaced with worksheets, desk time, and smart board lessons. My teaching time was forced to be less interactive, and I ended up dealing with more pretesting and post-testing material than actual learning content. My students struggled with learning empathy, compassion, and conflict resolution skills. These social emotional skills were given almost zero attention, with my teacher meetings solely focused on who was below, meeting, or exceeding standard… not about personal growth or improvement on a spectrum. Administrations never investigated the why's behind a third grader reading at a kindergarten level and the numbers and grades that did seem to matter didn't take into account real-life situations that impacted learning. I wanted to tend to a child's heart, not see them as a student identification number with a low test score.

I wanted to have a balance of all the things that mattered to me in teaching and to throw out the things that didn't, like test taking and the days I spent writing report cards. I took my areas of discontent, pondered them, considered what it would mean to dispose of the waste, and imagined what would be left: the golden nuggets of what I felt education could be. I started to think seven generations forward. What would students who went through a different kind of education system be like in ten years? What skills and knowledge would they need to be leaders and change makers? How could I, as a teacher, use my power and influence to create a just and more balanced world?

I worked through these questions while I was pregnant with my first child. I was alone, as Jose was still in Guatemala. The baby's timeline was not in sync with the timeline for Jose's Visa application. So, while our baby grew inside me, and as Jose continued to wait for approval so he could join us in the U.S., I went to prenatal classes with friends and had a baby blessing with loved ones. We arranged for a videographer and friends to keep Jose updated during the birth, wanting to ensure he could be there with us, in any way he could, when our baby finally joined us.

Keats, my first child, finally met his father in Guatemala seven months after he was born. While Keats and I were in Guatemala, Jose had his Visa appointment and was finally granted permission to return home to the U.S. with us. It was serendipitous because at Jose's first interview, the immigration officer flipped through the photos Jose gathered as evidence of our family. The officer wasn't very convinced, though, and asked for even more photos than we'd provided. Jose told them, "My family is here visiting right now." The next day, Keats and I joined Jose as his appointment. I held my breath as the officer flipped through my passport, asking me questions about dates and events. Then, before we knew it, *bam!* went the heavy stamp approving Jose's Visa! On August 20th, Jose took his first-ever flight. I watched him nervously make the sign of the cross over his head and heart as the plane took flight and headed for Tacoma. What a life-changing event, to leave everything he knew, all his family, and fly into the horizon toward a new life with his baby and wife. What trust that must have taken.

In the two years that followed, Jose stayed home to care for Keats while I taught at Geiger. The two of them would play at Play to Learn sessions with other moms and one other dad. Jose and Keats would take the city bus to town and walk down the neighborhood sidewalks to a local park. It worked out well for Jose to stay home while I continued my job. It gave him and Keats time to get used to this new world.

Then, after Keats' second birthday, we started looking into preschool options for him. It was important that Keats remain connected to his Spanish language, remain bilingual, learn outdoors, and that he wouldn't be the only mixed-race child in his program. I wanted him to experience preschool with other children who looked like him. No matter how hard we looked, though, we didn't find what our family needed.

At the same time, I realized my stress level from work continued to rise. The administrative and curriculum demands were never ending. And, overall, I was dissatisfied with my job. I craved reconnection with the earth and spent more of my time outside. I needed a different education option for Keats and myself, too. This was the catalyst for my dream to level-up my life and that of my family's lives. My dissatisfaction and Keat's budding need created the perfect opportunity to take all my favorite flavors of education and our family values and mix them together into something new. I added a few cups of reminiscing about my childhood, being outdoors, listening to trees, stomping through mud, and being in awe of a caterpillar to the recipe. Then, I added a few gallons of cultural diversity with Spanish language and other mixed-raced children. Plus a few pounds of being a space where my immigrant husband could use his teaching skills as a PE teacher in Guatemala. And finally, I included a few tablespoons of deep desire for something new. We mixed it all together, tasted and adjusted, shared taste tests with friends, and came up with the perfect new creation for our whole family: Chavitos Nature School.

After talking to many friends, parents, and teachers, we realized the next step to bring this creation to fruition would be finding the perfect location. One of my current students spoke often of a forest next to her home, which was just down the street from where our family lived. Jose and I went to check it out. The fence was broken down and open, allowing us easy access. I stepped into the space and knew instantly that this was the ideal location for our nature school. The area was just under a square acre in size, with over fifty old Douglas Firs and

rhododendrons. As it turned out, Jose and I knew the family who owned the land. They were a family who attended Geiger and had children in the age group I taught. I knew I had to build up the courage to share my business idea of an outdoor preschool with them. I dragged my heels on doing so but was lucky enough to have friends who confronted me about this. They asked, "Have you asked them yet? Why not?" That's when I realized I was scared. Not scared that the family would say no but terrified they would say *yes* and my whole life would be directed down a different path than what we were currently on. This decision would be life-changing for us, and it lay in the hands of other people.

To gain courage, I visualized the conversation I wanted to have with the owners. I imagined where, how, and what I would say. On the playground at pick up after school, I would say, "Hello Brook! We want to start a nature preschool on your property. We would love to barter rent with Spanish lessons, yard work, and taking care of your chickens."

When I finally held the conversation with the owners, it manifested exactly like I'd practiced! And soon after, we exchanged ideas over dinner one night. Since that day, we have had a peaceful, easeful connection with that family for nine years and our outdoor preschool program is still on that land. It has been an incredible, life sustaining connection for our family and community, and mutually beneficial for everyone involved. We continue to barter with the landowners for building projects, home repairs, yard projects, and more. We haven't paid any money for using the property. Instead, we steward the land and nurture a strong, mutually beneficial community connection with the owners.

We then secured use of the land through a permit, and in 2015, we opened Chavitos Nature School on a halftime preschool schedule. We offered morning preschool for eight students per class. Jose and I would teach there, together, in the mornings. Then, Jose would walk three kids home for lunch and play time. He supported friends whose work schedules needed our support. We bartered a weekly meal, usually quiche and rice, in exchange. Meanwhile, I continued to work part-time at the Montessori school in the afternoons, teaching literacy. After class, I would change from rain gear and Bog boots into my fancy teaching clothes to go to work with twigs and leaves in my hair. We kept that schedule for our first year in business and deeply enjoyed how our values led us to such an amazing job.

Our school was, and continues to be, bilingual Spanish-English. It is spearheaded by Jose, who is a native Spanish speaker and has a professional background in early childhood education and physical education. Together, Jose and I founded our nature school around our unique personal and professional giftings, which makes our school interesting to potential families. The second year we were open, our waitlist grew longer, and we took that as a sign to expand to two daily preschool sessions. I remember, each time we got an email with a new waitlist application, I was over the moon. It was such a rewarding experience to be able to give families what they need. And each new family seemed like a gift to us.

Mixed with that excitement of success was also my deep hesitation and fear around leaving my steady income and health benefits to start teaching at Chavitos full-time. *What if Chavitos doesn't work out?* I thought. *What if we aren't full? How the heck do I get self-employed health benefits? Will Keats enjoy being outdoors for six and a half hours in the winter? Heck, will I be able to do that?* Despite my hesitation, I received divinely timed and clear advice from my current principal at Geiger. After sharing my hesitancy, my principal responded, "Of course you need to try this. You're a free spirit and if you don't, you will regret it. You can always come back if it doesn't work out. You would be hired anywhere with your teaching record and high observation scores." His words were the affirmation I needed to hear. I left Geiger Montessori and since then, have taught, directed, and served in admin positions at Chavitos with Jose right by my side, entertaining my latest wildest dream (which changes frequently after I manifest whatever my current dream is).

One of those dreams came to fruition two years later, in 2017. I had just given birth to our second, chunky baby, Chano, who was born at home just three blocks from the forest school. Chano's first day at school was in late February and it was snowing. My maternity leave substitute was sick, and Jose had called everyone on our sub list. No one was available. Unwillingly, I bundled Chano up and wore her all day. We had a surprisingly lovely day, and I was reminded of what an incredible job and lifestyle we had created for ourselves and our growing family.

Not only were we growing babies, but we were growing financially, as well, with a steady income of monthly tuition. I knew it was time to implement our second dream: living in Guatemala for six months of the year. Since Jose had moved to Tacoma, we'd spent many of our family vacations returning to Guatemala. Chano took their first steps in the same central plaza in Antigua where Jose and I fell in love. Keats picked blackberries with Tio Carlos on walks there.

Sometimes, we would spend a few weeks at a time in Guatemala. But more often, we would stay for a month, volunteering and scouting out places we wanted to live for a longer timeframe or a permanent move. During one of those month-long stays, we volunteered at a Montessori school called Opal House in the hills above Lake Atitlan. Jose's friend, Francisco, picked us up to spend the night with his friend's family in Santiago, Atitlan. Something about that place, maybe the slightly larger village size than where we usually stayed, or the birds embroidered on the clothing and painted on the house walls, captured my heart. I declared, "When we return to Guatemala for six months, I want to live here!'

Just like with my other dreams, this dream was eventually manifested through hard work and patience. Back in Tacoma, we hired guides for six months, prepared our families for our absence, sublet the home we rented, and packed a lot of gifts for our family in Guatemala. When we finally arrived in Guatemala for our extended stay, our children attended a fantastic school called La Puerta Abierta. We had the privilege of living in a small pueblo with Indigenous people, and it was there, in Guatemala, that I realized I wanted to live my life according to a rhythm more aligned with nature, rather than the fast-paced rhythms of modern society.

Living in Guatemala was a dream, but it also challenged our family. It made us aware of our privilege from American culture, and we had to adjust to new ways of living each time we returned. Keats was afraid to sleep unless we looked under his bed for scorpions each night. The water quality is inconsistent, and we often have stomach issues from consuming water. When we used to visit, we'd have to stay in a two-room home with only one door.

In the U.S., our kids had the privilege of cloth diapers, new shoes, and unbroken toys and books. This led to conversations about how they could share their privilege with the neighborhood kids in Guatemala who wanted to play with their soccer ball and toys. We held conversations around the difference between necessities and wants. We also had conversations with our children about the beauty of being surrounded by a language completely foreign to them. One that is not Spanish or English, but the Indigenous language of Kaqchikel and Tz'utujil.

I loved that my children and I experienced all this together. Living in Guatemala seasonally allowed us to remain deeply connected to Jose's culture, and it is through this culture-bearing that we remain connected to one of our foundational beliefs as a family: we live simply and resourcefully. When we live within our means, we aren't thrown off or derailed as easily in life because our systems are sustainable. Living in Guatemala taught us the beauty of a seasonal market, a fast tuk-tuk, a near-empty fridge. It made us grateful for what we had available that day and made us aware of how little it takes to make us happy and whole.

During our second stint of living in Guatemala for six months, my dream wheels started to whirl again. Keats was growing into a first grader, and we realized we needed a new alternative to homeschooling and world-schooling for him. I started to visualize an elementary program built on the same foundations and values that made the preschool so successful. Jose sighed but agreed. He has been a constant supporter of physically manifesting my dreams and he is also my most beloved sounding board.

When we returned to the U.S., we started a small elementary program with a co-op of friends who taught different subjects at their homes. Melissa taught cooking and moon celebrations. Karen taught math and urban gardening in her hydroponics garden. Matt taught yoga and music. I taught literacy and Jose taught Spanish. Reflecting, this co-op, called Village, had some key factors we use today in our current K-8 program at Chavitos. It was there that we also added a two-day-a-week elementary program for students.

This successful rendition led us to start an official elementary school on a small property sitting on a hill overlooking China Lake in September 2018. I called it Chavitos on the Hill. After one successful year, I pocketed our successes, including a morning lake walk where students observed the lake in frozen form in the winter and dried lakebed in the early fall. I also pocketed the disasters, like a failed and quickly ended partnership with the owners of the property, and therefore the urgent need to relocate after our first year there. We also had under-qualified guides who had too much responsibility and not enough training and support from me. With these lessons, we realized we needed to buy our own property for security and longevity. We couldn't keep moving and establishing our program. For goodness' sake, we had a 630-pound, 16-foot geodome from Pacific Domes that Jose had to deconstruct and rebuild each time!

Then, a miracle occurred when, in early August of that year, we found a farm in Puyallup, Washington. The farm was owner-financed and had the infrastructure and space we needed. Again, I returned to all the lessons, experiences, and successful guiding values of my past. I drew strength, knowledge, and insight from them to craft our new program. Jose did the same and offered his skills in building and construction to turn the land we were on into a working farm. I spoke aloud about what needed to happen: a mound here for running a water feature; a whiteboard here for lessons; a goat and chicken pen there to teach the children about animals. Jose was quick to build, and it was a good thing, because we only had three weeks to complete it all. In that time, we hauled boulders to build the foundation and held interviews for guides on site. We hired the guides we needed. This time, we hired certified teachers with lots of classroom experience. I made sure to specifically inquire about their personal conflict style and how they would respond to challenging students. We finalized enrollment and supplies days before we started the program.

The elementary program, now a K-8 program, is an extension of the values we teach at Chavitos, but with more structure and depth than previous iterations. When creating the schedule, I included classes like marimba and social justice. We offer a balance of high-standard academics and engage a broad spectrum of elective classes. We weave holistic and child-led practices into our educational framework.

If you've read the other chapters of this book, you already know the struggles that accompanied this new location. It was devastating for us to learn that owning our property didn't make it any more secure a location. Also, hiring qualified teachers didn't prevent conflict and interpersonal crises. But, when examining what was working, the heart and rhythm of what we were offering at this location was hugely successful. My kids, returning enrollment rates, and guide retention were all indicators of our success.

And, as kids do, my kids kept growing and so did our dreams. Keats finished fifth grade, and the community started to dream about what middle school would look like for him and other children in our group. Once again, just like when he and his friends were two years old, I couldn't find what I wanted for our children. So, my visionary wheels began spinning again and I started to think of what a middle school-aged program could look like. This time, I got to do that dreaming with other parents, as we were then operating more as a co-op with parents actively sitting in circle with me and all of us making decisions together.

However, when I first shared the middle school idea with Jose, we were still in the muck of the unwelcoming neighbors and permitting issues at the farm. He flat out refused. No way was he going to start a third program, he said. Keats could go to public school. Jose wasn't onboard. But, as usual with Jose, he just needed a little time to adjust to the idea and accept a wild dream of mine. He eventually supported the idea after our middle school visionary meeting was a community-wide success.

I knew expanding to a third program meant I would have to be less involved with day-to-day teaching activities. I was already at my max with my current Chavitos responsibilities of director for preschool and elementary programs, farm manager, administrator for the preschool, and literacy and social justice guide for the elementary. I knew I needed to find the perfect support to make this work. I found myself in a vulnerable space, emotionally, as I needed to trust our vision and values to someone else (especially since my child would be involved). But I had also outgrown some of my duties and they didn't bring me joy anymore. I was ready to pass them along to someone else. So, I hired a director of middle school and a co-director for the elementary program. Now I have a leadership team who plans, advises, and solves problems with me weekly. I can't tell you what a shift this brought to my mental health.

2025 will be our first year of officially having a middle school program. Our middle school students gave themselves the name, "The Alphas," and I'm so excited to see what this project based, practical life program will be like for them. What successes will we pocket and continue? What challenges will we experience for the second year? I can't wait to find out. Whatever chapter of life and schooling we are in, we will bring our values of authenticity, belonging, age-appropriate expectations, community focus, and seasonal and connected life lessons based around nature's rhythms together to guide us along our path, the Chavitos Way.

Sources

Aloha Foundation. (2020, May 7). *A Mindful Way to Reflect: Rose, Thorn, and Bud.* Retrieved from https://alohafoundation.org/a-mindful-way-to-reflect-rose-thorn-and-bud

Brown, B. (2018). *Dare to Lead: Brave work. Tough conversations. Whole hearts.* Random House.

Burgess, R., & White, C. (2019). *Fibershed: Growing a movement of farmers, fashion activists, and makers for a new textile economy.* Chelsea Green Publishing.

Clark-Jackson, Y. (2024, July 2). *The Revolutionary Power of Grieving in Public.* Retrieved from *Yes! Magazine:* https://www.yesmagazine.org/health-happiness/2024/07/02/public-healing-grief

Csikszentmihalyi, M. (1990). *Flow: The psychology of optimal experience.* Harper & Row.

Curtice, K. B. (2023). *Living Resistance: An Indigenous vision for seeking wholeness every day.* Brazos Press.

Dennen, B. (2003). Peacing it together. In *Children's Songs for Peace and a Better World.* The Mosaic Project.

Doyle, G. (2020). *Untamed.* The Dial Press.

Gardner, H. (2011). *Frames of Mind: The Theory of Multiple Intelligences (3rd ed.).* New York: Basic Books.

Gray, P. (2013). *Free to Learn: Why unleashing the instinct to play will make our children happier, more self-reliant, and better students for life.* New York: Basic Books.

Maunz, M. (2022, May). *The Power of Hands-On Learning.* Retrieved from Montessori Foundation: https://www.montessori.org/the-power-of-hands-on-learning/

Ross, J., & Ghadbian, W. (2020). *Turning Towards Each Other: A conflict workbook.* Retrieved from https://96cd8e90-7f87-4399-af6b-c7156e91189a.filesusr.com/ugd/05f4b7_cec53ab03dcd4f32b1fecaf66ede2d80.pdf

Severson, K. (2020, June 17). *If Babies and Toddlers Can Detect Race, Why Do So Many Parents Avoid Talking about It?* Retrieved from Boston University: https://www.bu.edu/articles/2020/if-babies-and-toddlers-can-detect-race-why-do-so-many-parents-avoid-talking-about-it/

Siegel, D. J., & Bryson, T. P. (2018). *The Yes Brain: How to cultivate courage, curiosity, and resilience in your child.* Random House.

Siegel, D., & Bryson, T. P. (2011). *The Whole-Brain Child: 12 revolutionary strategies to nurture your child's developing mind.* Delacorte Press.

The Basics. (n.d.). Retrieved from National Institute for Play: https://nifplay.org/what-is-play/the-basics/

Thunberg, G. (2019, September 23). *Greta Thunberg's Speech At The U.N. Climate Action Summit.* Retrieved from PBS NewsHour: https://www.pbs.org/newshour/world/read-climate-activist-greta-thunbergs-speech-to-the-un

Whyte, D. (2015). *Consolations: The solace, nourishment and underlying meaning of everyday words.* Many Rivers Press.

Additional Resources

Chavitos Agreements

We hold agreements with children in our care. Children learn agreements at different times. Not all kids will learn agreements in one day, but usually, within a few days, most children know the procedure. Sometimes, with neurodivergent kids, it takes longer. But these children still gradually learn the same lessons. Because our program doesn't rush to begin or end things, we have the time to let things naturally happen. This is a great way to honor children's bodies and the diversity of the forest and families.

We have a special book that reiterates certain lessons to children. The goal of our program isn't that children do academics or learn to read the book, it's more about putting boundaries around social interaction and moral intelligence. This sounds like following agreements even when we don't want to. Here are some of the agreements we ask children to follow in our programs.

General Agreements

- **We follow ease and flow.** How can we make things easier for ourselves? By making routines and rituals for our community.

- **We acknowledge, not praise.** We acknowledge when children accomplish hard things. We acknowledge children's growth. "You put your backpack away. I can see from the smile on your face that you are proud," we might tell a child. This is acknowledgment, not praise. Praise is empty. Phrases like, "Good job. You're so smart!" leads to performance-based behavior. Acknowledging, conversely, is intrinsic. *I was tired but I still got up today. I made the effort. I can* *do this. I don't need stickers or candy or high fives,* we might think to ourselves, with our motivation coming from within. We want our children to be intrinsically motivated like this.

- **We don't have names on cubbies where children leave their gear.** That's counter to our way of being. We don't own space.

- **Children wait until a tool, toy, or natural element is available.** Whoever is on the swing can take as long as they want. If there's a line, we encourage patience for those waiting and the student on the swing is asked to look at the line and consider the other kids' feelings. At the swing, we see kids begin to try to control the situation. "You have two more minutes!" we hear them say. When this happens, guides jump into the conversation and identify feelings. "I see you really want a turn on the swing!"

- **Children can share something they've written or want to express in the author's chair.** They know everyone gets a turn. Each child learns to listen, and they learn to think about others. They learn their voices and stories matter. "You really want to share your writing with the class!" a guide might say. "You've been working on it for a whole month." Or, "You seem frustrated. Share how you feel." We guide children through sharing their feelings. This gives the other person they're engaging with clear communication, and it gives children the power to find resolution by themselves. It gives guides less work. This also leads to being able to engage in conflict resolution in any situation. Whether a child is at home with a sibling, a friend at a park, or with a parent.

Safety Agreements

Safety agreements show up as mantras in the forest. I envision the Agreements that follow (and distill) every chapter becoming the mantras that parents and guides can carry into their lives and impart on their children.

- Big sticks in big places.
- You make it, you break it.
- Branches bigger than the width of our arms.
- Check the branch? Is it ready to hold your weight?
- If the toy is being used, the toy is not available.
- Listen to your body. What does it need?
- We can do hard things!

Self-Reliance Agreements

- **We hang up our backpacks by ourselves.** If a child's bag is too heavy, parents should reconsider what they pack inside it.

- **Get yourself in or out of the tree.** We won't do it for you, though we will offer you guidance. If a child asks us to get in or out of a tree, they are not ready to climb that tree. We say, "I can't do that. That's your work. But you can practice on a smaller tree. Then you'll be able to do the bigger tree before you know it." Our climbing limits at the school are as high as a guide can raise their arms above their hands.

Recommended Reading List

Braiding Sweetgrass by Robin Wall Kimmerer

The Children's Forest by Dawn Casey, Anna Richardson, and Helen d' Ascoli

Coyote Guide by Jon Young

How to Talk so Little Kids Listen by Joanna Faber and Julie King

How to Raise an Antiracist by Ibram X Keni

Last Child in the Woods by Richard Louv

Living Resistance by Kaitlin B. Curtice

Mending Life: A Handbook for Repairing Clothes and Hearts
    by Nina Montenegro and Sonya Montenegro

The Mosaic Project

Piecing it Together by Brett Dennen

Seven Times the Sun: Guiding Your Child Through the Rhythms of the Day
    by Shea Darian

This Book is Anti-racist by Tiffany Jewel

Turning Towards Each Other by Jovida Ross and Weyam Ghadbian

The Whole Brain Child by Daniel J Siegel and Tina Payne Bryson

About the Author

Meag Diamond is a Cedarsong certified Forest Kindergarten teacher. For 17 years she has taught in the public and private school environments in Washington and in Lagos, Nigeria. Before starting Chavitos, she spent six years at a local public Montessori school as a Lower Elementary Teacher. Meag holds her National Board Certification in Literacy and also possesses a Montessori certification.

Meag is passionate about plant medicine and social justice. She has started growing herbal medicine in her wild garden and uses them in her home apothecary. She and her husband tend to land and have been learning to align with the land's vision and destiny. Meag dreams about helping others start their own nature-based education schools.

About the Press

Vega Books is an imprint of Blue Cactus Press, an independent publisher. Our mission is to craft books and experiences that spark dialogue about liberation. Our books are written and crafted by people from historically marginalized groups. We believe books can be used as tools for dreaming new worlds and realities into existence, and for bridging the gap between words and action.

We envision a world in which books empower & celebrate communities we walk in. We strive to implement equitable business models that center collective liberation as the rule, not the exception, and offer makers dignity, autonomy, and creative voice in our practices. We work toward a future in which our planet is prioritized over profit and publishing practices are accessible and gate-free.

We seek creatively satisfying, financially viable, and relationally resonant work. We value curiosity, craftsmanship, and relational responsibility among humans, our environment, and other living organisms.

To support the press, please request our books at libraries, become a member at **patreon.com/bluecactuspress** or purchase our books at **bluecactuspress.com**.

www.ingramcontent.com/pod-product-compliance
Lightning Source LLC
Chambersburg PA
CBHW052112030426

42335CB00025B/2945